1996

Common Values

The Paul Anthony Brick Lectures

The Paul Anthony Brick Lectureship was made possible by a generous bequest from Paul Anthony Brick in 1948 to "develop the science of ethics." The lectureship established with that bequest provides for an annual or biennial series of lectures on ethics to be given at the University of Missouri. The guidelines for the lectures stipulate that they are to address a general audience but should be presented by a scholar with an established reputation. In addition, "The subject matter of the lectureship shall be determined broadly, including ethics not merely in the technical and philosophical sense but also in its relations to literature, society, religion, and other phases of contemporary culture."

Common

Values

Sissela Bok

University of Missouri Press ■ *Columbia and London*

Library of Congress Cataloging-in-Publication Data

Bok, Sissela.
    Common values / Sissela Bok.
       p. cm.—(The Paul Anthony Brick lectures)
    Essays originally given as lectures and later published in journals, 1990–1995.
    Includes bibliographical references and index.
    ISBN 0-8262-1038-4 (alk. paper)
    1. Values. 2. Ethics. 3. Social Values.   I. Title. II. Series.
BD232.B595   1996
170—dc20   95-25333
                                                       CIP

Designer: Stephanie Foley
Typesetter: BOOKCOMP
Printer and binder: Thomson-Shore, Inc.
Typefaces: Gill Sans and Palatino

Contents

Acknowledgments

The chapters in this book are based on lectures given and essays published between 1988 and 1994. The first chapter originated as the Brick Lecture at the University of Missouri–Columbia in April 1994. I am most grateful to all who offered comments at the time, and greatly valued the opportunity to meet with members of the University of Missouri community during my visit, as well as the kind hospitality that met me from the moment I arrived. In reworking my Brick Lecture for publication, I have had the opportunity to take into account the suggestions made at that time as well as during other presentations of the material contained in the other four chapters. I thank commentators at the Chautauqua Institution, New York, and Williams College for their responses to earlier versions of Chapter 1, and those at Columbia University, FA-Rådet, Stockholm, and the Common Security Forum meeting at Tokai University in Tokyo, Japan, for discussions of partially overlapping drafts.[1]

Chapters 2, 3, 4, and 5 also originated as lectures at a number of institutions. They were then published as, respectively: "The Search for a Shared Ethics," *Common Knowledge* (winter 1992); "What Basis for Morality? A Minimalist Approach," *The Monist* (July 1993); "Early Advocates of Lasting World Peace: Utopians or Realists?" *Ethics and International Affairs* (1990), reprinted in Joel H. Rosenthal,

1. One of these drafts was published as "Cultural Diversity and Shared Moral Values," in Lincoln Chen and Tatsuro Matsumae, eds., *Common Security Forum in Asia: New Concept of Human Security* (Tokyo: Tokai University, 1995); another is forthcoming as "Shared Moral Values," in Hans de Geer and Gunilla Silfverberg, ed., *Citizens' Trust and Authorities' Choices*, a report from the Fourth International Conference on Ethics in the Public Service, Stockholm, June 15–18, 1994, forthcoming.

ed., *Ethics and International Affairs: A Reader* (Washington, D.C.: Georgetown University Press, 1995), 150–68; "Complex Humanitarian Emergencies: Moral Quandaries," *Medicine and Global Survival* 1 (December 1994).

I am grateful to the editors of these publications for their assistance and for permission to reprint these articles. The first article, originally published in *Common Knowledge,* is also reproduced here by permission of Oxford University Press. Each article has been updated, coordinated, and considerably revised for the present volume. I thank my colleagues at the Stanford, California, Center for Advanced Study of the Behavioral Sciences, in 1991–1992, at the Joan Barone Shorenstein Center for the Press, Politics, and Public Policy at Harvard University, in 1993, and at the Harvard Center for Population and Development Studies, beginning in 1993, for stimulating discussions of many of the issues raised in these chapters.

In addition, I thank all who offered comments at workshops at which I presented the material that went into these essays, as well as at lectures on the following occasions: Barnard University's Centennial, 1989; the Ware Lecture at the Unitarian-Universalist General Assembly in New Haven, 1989; Princeton University, 1989; the American Philosophical Association, 1990; the Connecticut College Sykes Memorial Lecture, 1992; Stanford University Ethics in Society Program, 1992; Stanford University Program in Security Studies, 1992; Case Western Reserve University Medical School, 1992; Presbyterian College, 1992; the Harvard Program for Ethics in the Professions, 1992; the North American Institute, Santa Fe, 1992; the Ford Hall Forum, Boston, 1992; the University of Maine at Portland, 1992; Iona College, 1993; Fordham University, 1993; Trinity College, Vermont, 1993; the University of Maine at Bangor, 1993; Simmons College, 1993; the Boston University Institute for Philosophy and Religion, 1993; the Harvard Center for Population and Development Studies, 1994.

I thank, also, participants at conferences and meetings at the University of Mexico, the University of Moscow, and the University of Oslo for exchanges on the subjects taken up in these essays. Among persons with whom I have talked over these subjects and corresponded about them, I want to thank, especially, Sudhir Anand,

Anthony Appiah, Robert Audi, Tom Beauchamp, Hilary Bok, Derek Bok, Daniel Callahan, Lincoln Chen, Diana Eck, Dagfinn Føllesdal, Neva Goodwin, Amy Gutmann, Stanley Hoffmann, Rushworth Kidder, Christine Korsgaard, Jennifer Leaning, Michael McPherson, Julius Moravçik, Martha Nussbaum, Susan Okin, Herbert Okun, Amélie Rorty, Emma Rothschild, LeRoy Rouner, Enid Schoettle, Amartya Sen, Adele Simmons, John Simon, Brita Stendahl, Krister Stendahl, Dennis Thompson, Margaret Walker, Tu Weiming, Lloyd Weinreb, David Wilkins, David Wong, and Nur Yalman for their suggestions and challenges, either with respect to specific aspects of my arguments or, over time, to all of them taken together.

Finally, I am most grateful to the staff at the University of Missouri Press for their assistance with successive drafts of the Brick Lecture and for their help in producing the entire book.

Common Values

Projects for worldwide ethics litter history like tanks abandoned in the desert. Utopian, grandiose, commonsensical, totalitarian—in our century, we have seen them all. By now, in the 1990s, when ethnic and religious conflicts devastate so many regions, it may seem especially quixotic to speak of values recognizable across cultural, religious, ethnic, and other boundaries—even downright offensive to many who stress fundamental value differences between North and South, Asia and the West, men and women, old and young, colonizers and indigenous peoples.

There is surely great need for caution about slogans invoking common values, often so glibly used to disguise efforts to proselytize and subdue. It is nevertheless urgent to seek out fundamental moral values on which to base cross-cultural dialogue and choice, given the nature and scope of the challenges societies now confront together. In what sense, then, and with what constraints, safeguards, and qualifications, might we best inquire into the prospects for a common ethics?

I suggest, in this book, that we look for a limited set of values so down-to-earth and so commonplace as to be most easily recognized across societal and other boundaries. To the extent that they are acknowledged as common and respected as such, they can provide a basis from which to undertake the dialogue and collaboration now needed. But they must also be so clear-cut as to offer standards for critiquing abuses—including those perpetrated either in the name of universalist political, religious, or moral doctrines or in that of ethnic, religious, political, or other diversity.

We have every reason to seek out such values and to inquire into the prospects for putting them to broader, more imaginative practical use in responding to challenges which, themselves, stop at no barriers, whether natural or humanly erected. We are nearing the end of our century with previously undreamed of possibilities for collaboration across every frontier and boundary, but also with problems of a severity and magnitude that call for unprecedented levels of such collaboration. Information, capital, travelers, and merchandise move across boundaries worldwide as never before. The same, however, is true of pollution, epidemics such as AIDS, famines, and natural disasters that recognize no cultural, ethnic, religious, or other barriers. Terrorists and traffickers in drugs and arms likewise have singular disregard for the niceties of passport controls and customs offices. Long-term environmental threats such as those of greenhouse warming or of damage to Earth's ozone layer concern the future of children everywhere, without regard to nationality, religion, or race. And humanitarian emergencies such as those in Rwanda or Bosnia can neither be contained within national frontiers nor fail to present policy choices to the entire international community.

These are interlocking worldwide challenges; surely the responses, to stand even a chance of being effective, must be collective as well, encouraging and coordinating efforts from the local to the state and international levels. We can no longer afford the stumbling and backsliding of this past century and earlier ones. Yet governments, aid agencies, and the international community have repeatedly temporized and acted at cross-purposes even when confronted with the most immediate and egregious crises, while societies are overtaken by misery or descend into barbarism, at times genocide.

The resulting public discouragement and sense of helplessness are great. They are augmented by consciousness of the sheer magnitude of the present threats to survival. As we approach the end of this century, the number of what the World Bank calls "the absolute poor" has climbed to over 1.3 billion. This represents a 50 percent increase since the late 1970s alone.[1] As many human beings now

---

1. The Commission on Global Governance, *Our Global Neighborhood* (Oxford: Oxford University Press, 1995), 21.

live in utter destitution as constituted Earth's entire population at the beginning of this century. More people are estimated to have died from war-related causes in this century than in all the preceding sixteen centuries since the Fall of Rome. Civilians are at greatest risk: whereas the proportion of civilian deaths among all war-related casualties was already a grotesquely high 50 percent four decades ago, it is now an unimaginable 90 percent.[2] Over 30 million people have been killed in wars and other conflicts in that period, and 40 million more are part of "an epidemic of mass migration."[3]

This vast expansion of human misery is paralleled, however, by even greater growth in the numbers of the well-to-do. During the course of our century, many societies have achieved unprecedented prosperity. Global levels of *average* longevity, nutrition, health, and literacy continue to climb. But the gap only widens between rich and poor, between those who can avail themselves of the world's expanding opportunities and those living at the edge of extinction: just in the last three decades, the income gap between the world's richest 20 percent and poorest 20 percent has doubled.[4]

This widening gap between haves and have-nots and the sheer magnitude and intensity of present suffering challenge, I suggest, all existing conceptions of human rights and duties and obligations. What does it mean in practice, under today's conditions, to speak of honoring human rights, of abiding by the Golden Rule, of taking seriously the duty to aid fellow humans in distress, or of upholding the legal obligation on governments to intervene to stop genocide? What does it mean to call for "launching a world crusade against mass poverty" or to speak of a "new global social contract"?[5]

2. Michael Renner, *Critical Juncture: The Future of Peacekeeping* (Washington, D.C.: Worldwatch Institute, 1993), 9.

3. "Effective Humanitarian Aid," editorial, *Journal of the American Medical Association* 270, no. 5 (1993): 632.

4. James Gustave Speth, chief of the United Nations Development Program, speaking at the United Nations World Summit for Social Development, March 6, 1995, quoted by Barbara Crossette, in "U.N. Parley Ponders How to Stretch Scarce Aid Funds," *New York Times,* March 7, 1995, A6.

5. Calls to action by James Speth and by U.N. Secretary General Boutros Boutros Ghali at the U.N. World Summit for Social Development, ibid.

Too easily, such language merely draws attention to a second widening gap, between rhetoric and reality. Struck by the discrepancy between high-flown phrases and inaction in the face of unspeakable brutality and suffering, many conclude that value claims are nothing but pointless slogans in today's world—a view that contributes further to their sense of uneasy helplessness in the face of the first gap.

The pressures on long-standing moral convictions are made still more immediate now that satellite television brings into living rooms the world over close-ups of the faces of starving children and of victims of persecution in crowded refugee camps. At the beginning of this century, news spread more slowly. Many calamities went unmentioned in the media, and information about others filtered forth only gradually. Today, natural disasters, military conflicts, human rights abuses, and humanitarian crises are presented ceaselessly on the world's television screens.

The result is a third widening gap: between mounting numbers both of the concerned and of the resolutely or anxiously indifferent. This gap, too, has to do with moral response. We hear of increasing numbers of individuals devoting themselves to aiding those in need and of the remarkable growth of nongovernmental organizations working the world over to assist communities and to foster development; but we also know of the growing "compassion fatigue" among citizens of richer nations and of the many individuals and governments prepared to click entire regions of the world off their screen.

How can we hope to bridge these three widening gaps—between haves and have-nots, rhetoric and reality, concern and indifference—that undercut all efforts to address the present stark challenges? It will not be possible to begin to do so, I suggest, without stressing a few widely acknowledged fundamental values that could provide a basis from which to undertake such bridging. Foremost among them are the constraints on violence and deceit recognized in every moral and religious tradition. True, these constraints have too rarely been thought to operate with respect to outsiders and enemies of a society or culture, least of all by those who view violence as legitimate for purposes of conquest or conversion; but once the constraints are recognized as fundamental everywhere, they offer common ground for cross-cultural debate and for collective responses to common threats.

I first examine past and present efforts to consider such values, taking my departure from the Brick Lecture that I gave at the University of Missouri–Columbia in April 1994. In revised form, this lecture constitutes Chapter 1 in this book, "Cultural Diversity and Common Values." I draw, in this chapter, on proposals in my book *A Strategy for Peace: Human Values and the Threat of War* for relying on the languages of both strategy and morality, long used separately to consider issues of war and peace and human survival. Both must now be seen as equally indispensable. We must draw on the traditions of moral as well as strategic reflection to consider how individuals, groups, and nations can best protect common goals of survival and flourishing, in the face of shared risks of unprecedented magnitude; and we can only do so on the basis of fundamental values recognized in both traditions.

In preparing to give the 1994 Brick Lecture, I was interested to see questions concerning common values explicitly set forth, debated, challenged, in the course of four quite different international inquiries into and statements about fundamental moral standards: the 1993 United Nations World Conference on Human Rights, in Vienna; the World Parliament of Religions, in Chicago in August 1993; *Veritatis Splendor,* Pope John Paul II's encyclical on morality, published in the fall of 1993; and the International Commission on Global Governance meeting that same year to begin preparing a statement on shared values, published early in 1995. I found it helpful to be able to examine the question of common values in the light of the four statements; and in turn to examine these statements from the point of view of how they dealt with that question.

The inquiries regarding common values that I discuss in Chapter 1 are subject to four important objections, advanced since antiquity in debates about such values, but newly and often cogently formulated in recent decades. Although two are primarily theoretical in nature, conclusions drawn on the basis of each of the four can do serious damage in practice to the chances for productive cross-cultural dialogue and cooperation. The same is true, however, of conclusions that fail to recognize the striking relevance of these objections for contemporary efforts to promote such dialogue and cooperation and the legitimate caution that each of the four ought therefore to inspire. I consider the four objections in Chapters 2–5.

The first of these objections is based on the time-honored skeptical doubt of all moral claims, including those regarding common human values. In "The Search for a Common Ethics" (Chapter 2), I address a contemporary version of this view: the challenge to the very idea of the possibility of shared values posed by anthropologists and other intellectuals, given all that we now know about human diversity.

In the years since the end of the Cold War, we have seen a striking contrast in this respect. On the one hand advocates such as Aung San Suu Kyi and Václav Havel were willing to risk everything for ideals of freedom, justice, and human dignity that they took to be universal. On the other hand, many intellectuals were standing aside from human problems at home or abroad on the ground that there can be no meaningful discourse about shared values or even understandings across cultural and linguistic boundaries. Their stance, I argue, is reminiscent of the *trahison des clercs* of which Julien Benda wrote in the 1920s. To counter the resulting passivity, I discuss the obstacles to recognizing a minimalist set of common values and consider the prospects for their being acknowledged, both as widely held and as calling for cross-cultural observance.

The second objection denies the claim that any values can be justified on similar grounds across all cultural boundaries. It, too, has ancient roots. But it has been discussed especially vigorously in recent decades, as our awareness of the world's many different justifications for values in different moral and religious traditions has grown. How can any set of values form an adequate basis for the kind of cross-cultural debate, dialogue, and collaboration that I take to be needed, so long as no common foundations or justifications can be specified for these values? I address this objection in Chapter 3, "What Basis for Morality? A Minimalist Approach." Among the types of justification most commonly advanced for moral values, I agree that none is likely to be held in common. Some invoke divine authority for those values, others see them as inscribed in human nature, still others as existing independently, perhaps as part of the natural order or as perceivable by a "moral sense." I conclude that although agreement on such foundations is indeed out of reach, this need in no way preclude relying on a minimalist set of basic values as a starting point for cross-cultural understanding, negotiation, and cooperation.

The third objection invokes Thucydides as the ancestor of "realist" views about the role of ethics in domestic and international affairs. It questions whether any set of common values could have much practical import, even if one could be identified in theory and set forth as the basis for cross-cultural dialogue. Many have thought it naive, possibly even counterproductive from the point of view of any nation's best interest, to take moral considerations into account in policy making. In Chapter 4, "Advocates of Lasting Peace: Utopians or Realists?," I respond to this third objection by considering the charge of utopianism leveled at those who, like Erasmus and Kant, have taken seriously the role of ethics at all levels of human interaction, including the international one. I compare the impoverishment, destruction, and mass death brought by armies and warring factions in societies such as Lebanon and Ethiopia with the astounding successes achieved by nonviolent means in Eastern Europe and elsewhere. And I argue that nonviolent resistance, combining moral constraints and strategic planning, is not only more respectful of human rights and less likely to brutalize and corrupt participants, but also capable of bringing speedier and more far-reaching results. It is preferable, therefore, on both strategic and moral grounds.

The difference between such an approach to conflicts and one that tramples on basic values grows more glaring as the ethnic and religious conflicts in Africa, the former Yugoslavia, and elsewhere devastate entire populations with no end in sight, even as adversaries in South Africa, Ireland, Cambodia, and the Near East work to achieve by peaceful means the mutual security that war could never bring. Not every effort at reconciliation succeeds. But I am convinced that the choice between the two approaches to human problems will do more to determine the fate of humanity than any conflicts between different religious worldviews or political systems or civilizations or ethnic groups. That contest between two approaches is now being waged *within* many religious and political traditions. The central question at issue is: Must nations and groups give in to partisanship leading them to violate the most fundamental moral constraints, and thereby endlessly reenact outmoded patterns of response to conflict, or can they, rather, combine strategy and ethics so as to promote their goals by other means?[6]

A fourth objection arises, however, to trouble even those who agree on the importance of common values. It concerns the well-known harm to which efforts to "do good" can unwittingly contribute. This is not an objection to such intentions in their own right so much as a recognition of human fallibility when it comes to carrying them out in practice. It has been explored by nearly all moral philosophers and religious thinkers and is dramatized anew by the humanitarian emergencies of the post–Cold War era. Large numbers of people have been moved by the desperate plight of victims of the many current wars and have given unprecedented amounts of relief money to UNICEF, the Red Cross, Care, and other organizations operating in the field to bring humanitarian aid. Many individuals the world over have enlisted in these organizations to bring food, shelter, water, and medications, or to work as health professionals, engineers, human rights observers, or technicians. Their contributions have been desperately needed and have often done much good. But at times, these workers have despaired to find their interventions helping to prolong a conflict, buttress repressive regimes, even legitimize genocidal local authorities.

Which is worst, under such circumstances? To leave, and thus abandon children and others who have done nothing to deserve such abandonment? Or to stay on, for their sake, and contribute to the perpetuation of war and repression? What does it really mean, in the field, to bring humanitarian aid? What *has* it meant, say in the prison camps for refugees from the genocidal conflict in Rwanda? Who is helped and who is hurt by such efforts? When does humanitarian aid actually prolong certain conflicts? Is friction bound to arise

---

6. See Sissela Bok, *A Strategy for Peace: Human Values and the Threat of War* (New York: Pantheon Books, 1989), 25.

between those who advocate greater respect for human rights and those who stress that priority be given to providing food and shelter wherever the need is greatest? How can one best combine both moral and strategic considerations in considering the excruciating problems that arise for individuals on the front lines in these aid efforts as well as for organizations and governments?

These are the questions that I address in Chapter 5, "Humanitarian Emergencies: Whose Rights? Whose Responsibilities?" As we near the end of a century in which the three gaps mentioned above—between haves and have-nots, rhetoric and reality, concern and indifference—continue to widen, the full scope and difficulty of these questions are only beginning to be taken into account in international and domestic debates. Answers still elude us, even as they elude the field workers and policy makers who confront these dilemmas daily. The search for answers will be central to the debate over the role of ethics in the century to come, engaging collaborators and adversaries the world over. They will have at least a starting point from which to begin to the extent that they acknowledge a minimalist set of common values.

Chapter I

Cultural Diversity
and Common Values

How can we formulate an ethics or a method of moral science which would serve the cause of morals for all mankind?

Herbert W. Schneider, *Morals for Mankind*

How is government to be carried on, if, lying behind it, there is no consensus morality? If there is, as we are often told now, no general shared sense of what is right and wrong, how are laws to be enacted? . . . And, if enacted, how are they to be enforced?

Mary Warnock, *The Uses of Philosophy*

D oes it make sense to envisage a morality shared across cultural, linguistic, and other barriers? In what sense can we still speak, as Herbert Schneider did in his inaugural Brick Lecture, of "morals for mankind"? Or even of what Mary Warnock refers to as "consensus morality" within a society?[1] And how, in speaking thus, can we also grant the fullest respect for cultural and other diversity? It is not possible, many argue, to insist on respecting both difference and sameness when it comes to moral values: on honoring individual and cultural diversity while also holding that certain moral values

1. Schneider, *Morals for Mankind* (Columbia: University of Missouri Press, 1960), 55; Warnock, *The Uses of Philosophy* (Oxford: Blackwell, 1992), 85.

go to the heart of what it means to be human and always have, since the beginning of time, and always must if we are not to lose touch with our humanity.

Such doubts are understandable. Too often in the past, those who have spoken of universal values have intended to impose their own religious and political value systems coercively as a pattern for all to adopt. And even in the absence of aims to dominate and conquer, we have to ask whether it is not simply naive to invoke common values or consensus morality, given the persecution and slaughter in so many parts of the world and the shrill voices inciting racial and religious violence in our own societies. Henry Louis Gates, Jr., writes of such incitements:

> "One million Arabs are not worth a Jewish fingernail," Rabbi Yaacov Perrin said in a funeral eulogy for Baruch Goldstein. The phrase reflects a perverse misreading of a passage from Exodus. But we have heard this voice before. It is the voice of messianic hatred. We hear it from the Balkans to the Bantustans; from Hezbollah and from Kach. We hear it in the streets of Bensonhurst, New York. And of course we hear it from some who profess to be addressing the misery of black America. "Never will I say I am not an anti-Semite," said Khalid Abdul Mohammed of the Nation of Islam. "I pray that God will kill my enemy and take him off the face of the planet Earth."[2]

Might it perhaps even be a form of cowardice to speak of values that can be shared and rights that must be respected everywhere, a flight into abstractions to avoid confronting the human realities attesting to moral incommensurability and dissonance? The very title of Dr. John Hope Franklin's 1993 Brick Lecture—*The Color Line*—speaks volumes about the distance between easy rhetoric about shared values and the bitter realities of racism and mutual suspicion; his lecture outlines the massive "good-faith effort to turn our history around" needed to break free of this pattern.[3]

---

2. "Living Together: For a Humanism That Cares to Speak Its Mind," *New York Times*, March 24, 1994.

3. *The Color Line: Legacy for the Twenty-First Century* (Columbia: University of Missouri Press, 1993), 74.

Others reject even that possibility. In his book *Civil Wars*, Hans Magnus Enzenberger, the German social critic, dismisses as worthless all references to universal values such as human rights. He sees the disintegration of all social and humane values spreading like a virus in cities and warring societies the world over: "Never has there been so much *talk* of human rights as now, nor has the number of people who know them only as a phrase ever been so large."[4] As the epidemic of violence spreads, he predicts that collective responses will be increasingly futile. The best that can be done, however inadequate, is to undertake whatever limited efforts at rebuilding may be possible at the local level.

How might we answer those who are ready to give up in this way and who dismiss all talk of common values as pointless if not outright cynical? I take their defeatism to be premature. It ignores the gap that has sprung up, in this century, between unprecedented numbers of both rich and poor: a gap that allows for vastly differing possible scenarios for future development. And to leap from the mounting toll taken by today's societal catastrophes to the worthlessness of efforts to combat violations of human rights is as simplistic as to conclude from the increase in victims of AIDS that preventive efforts and research into cures for this disease are pointless. The present egregious denials of human rights reveal the horrors possible once the fabric of common values tears or is ripped apart; but surely this proves nothing about the futility of collective efforts to repair and reverse the damage.

To explain the crucial role that I see for common values in such efforts, I shall advance four propositions:

1. Certain basic values necessary to collective survival have had to be formulated in every society. A minimalist set of such values can be recognized across societal and other boundaries.

---

4. *Civil Wars* (New York: New Press, 1994), 66–71. To be sure, Enzenberger affirms that most people everywhere would wish to be free from persecution, torture, threats to life, and lawlessness—freedoms that constitute "the minimum prerequisites of civilization"—but as he looks back at the history of humanity, he takes this minimum to have been achieved "only exceptionally and temporarily" (138). He views as the true "common denominators" at present, rather, the characteristics of all who take part in the spreading civil wars: the autistic nature of the perpetrators, their inability to distinguish between destruction and self-destruction, and their seeing no need to legitimize violence (20).

2. These basic values are indispensable to human coexistence, though far from sufficient, at every level of personal and working life and of family, community, national, and international relations.

3. It is possible to affirm both common values and respect for diversity and in this way to use the basic values to critique abuses perpetrated in the name either of more general values or of ethnic, religious, political, or other diversity.

4. The need to pursue the inquiry about which basic values can be shared across cultural boundaries is urgent, if societies are to have some common ground for cross-cultural dialogue and for debate about how best to cope with military, environmental, and other hazards that, themselves, do not stop at such boundaries.

Four Propositions

1. Certain basic values necessary to collective survival have had to be formulated in every society. A minimalist set of such values can be recognized across societal and other boundaries.

Not all societies have developed ideals such as those of liberty, equality, or the sanctity of life, much less identical ones. The same is true of views regarding religious faiths or political systems, not to mention the rules regarding diet, clothing, and sexuality that differ so greatly among societies. What values, then, can lay claim to being more universally present in spite of the differences on so many other scores? I suggest that there are three categories of values so fundamental to group survival that they have had to be worked out in even the smallest community.

A. All human groups, first of all, and all religious, moral, and legal traditions stress some form of positive duties regarding mutual support, loyalty, and reciprocity. Children have to be reared and the wounded, weak, and sick tended. As the Roman thinker Cicero puts it, nature brings human beings together for purposes of survival and implants in them "a strangely tender love" for their offspring.[5]

5. Cicero, *De Officiis (Of Duties)* (44B.C.), book 1.

Many traditions—Judeo-Christian, Muslim, Confucian, Buddhist, and Hindu among them—also expressly enjoin children to obey and honor their parents. For instance, when the Buddhist emperor Asoka caused three central moral guidelines to be carved on a pillar in central India in the third century B.C., the first one was "Father and mother must be obeyed."[6]

The injunctions to honor and obey parents and to offer other forms of family and group support differ greatly in scope; even the most limited ones are too often outrageously violated in practice. Otherwise they would not need to be stated as injunctions and commandments. But any community in which they were altogether lacking would be short-lived. And as Mary Midgley points out, there is a stress on reciprocity in the provision of such support: "in all existing moralities, [it appears] not just as insurance for the future but as appropriate gratitude owed for kindness showed in the past, and as flowing naturally from the affection that goes with it."[7]

Midgley agrees with Darwin that humans take their departure from the disposition they share with many animal species to provide mutual care and support and that their being also endowed with memory and intelligence is what makes long-range planning possible. These powers, along with the effects of habit and the social instincts, Darwin held, "naturally lead to the Golden Rule."[8]

The Golden Rule has been formulated, the world over, either positively, as an injunction to "do unto others as you would have them do unto you" (Matthew 7:12), or negatively, urging that you not do to others what you would not wish them to do to you, as in the sayings of Confucius or Hillel. In either formulation, the Golden

6. Emperor Asoka's Second Minor Rock Edict continues: "likewise a respect for all life must be an established principle; truth must be spoken." Radhakumud Mookerji, *Asoka* (Delhi: Motilal Banarsidass, 1962), 116.

7. "The Origin of Ethics," in Peter Singer, ed., *A Companion to Ethics* (Oxford: Blackwell, 1990), 3–13, at 10–11. See also George Silberbauer, "Ethics in Small-Scale Societies," ibid., 14–28.

8. "The Origin of Ethics," 10. Charles Darwin, *The Descent of Man* (1859; Princeton: Princeton University Press, 1981), 106. See also the discussion of Darwin's and Midgley's views, and of the origins of ethics, in Peter Singer, *The Expanding Circle* (New York: Farrar, Strauss, Giroux, 1981).

Rule represents not so much a moral value or principle in its own right as a perspective necessary to the exercise of even the most rudimentary morality: that of trying to put oneself in the place of those affected by one's actions, so as to counter the natural tendency to moral myopia.[9]

B. The second category of fundamental values consists of negative duties to refrain from harmful action. All societies have stressed certain basic injunctions against at least a few forms of wronging other people—chief among these "force and fraud," or violence and deceit. From the Ten Commandments to Buddhist, Jain, Confucian, Hindu, and many other texts, violence and deceit are most consistently rejected, as are the kinds of harm they make possible, such as torture and theft. To cement agreement about how and when these curbs apply, and to keep them from being ignored or violated at will, another negative injunction is needed—against breaches of valid promises, contracts, laws, and treaties. Together these injunctions, against violence, deceit, and betrayal, are familiar in every society and every legal system. They have been voiced in works as different as the Egyptian Book of the Dead, the Icelandic Edda, and the Bhagavad-Gita.

As with the positive injunctions to reciprocity and mutual support in the first category of basic values mentioned above, the negative ones, too, have been frequently violated within most communities and have often been thought not to apply at all with respect to outsiders. Such violations have been held most excusable, at times justifiable, when seen to promote survival, as in the use of force or deceit in self-defense; but within societies, long-term group survival has called for their constraint. As a result, all communities, no matter how small or disorganized, no matter how hostile toward outsiders, no matter how cramped their perception of what constitutes, say, torture, have to impose at least *some* internal curbs on violence, deceit, and betrayal in order to survive.[10]

9. See my entry on the Golden Rule in *The Oxford Companion to Philosophy* (Oxford: Oxford University Press, forthcoming).

10. See *A Strategy for Peace: Human Values and the Threat of War* (New York: Pantheon Books, 1989), chaps. 2 and 4.

Onora O'Neill argues that these curbs lie at the basis of principles that can be coherently adopted, or universalized, in any society. Principles of deception, coercion, and violence cannot be universalized, she holds, if one bases universalization on the "traditional, minimal, formal sense" of justice as like requirements for like cases: "justice demands (at least) that actions and institutions not be based on principles of victimization (deception, coercion, violence.)"[11]

C. A third category of basic values worked out in all societies consists of norms for at least rudimentary fairness and procedural justice in cases of conflict regarding both positive and negative injunctions, prominently including those listed in the first two categories above. Views regarding the modalities of justice differ, as do legal systems; but all societies share certain fundamental procedures for listening to both sides and determining who is right and who is wrong in disputes. Thus, in working out the basics of fairness, every known society with rules for trials has rejected the bearing of false witness—something that vitiates a fair trial from the outset.[12] Likewise, all societies have some rule of "treating as equal what is equal under the accepted system," just as it is everywhere perceived as unfair, from childhood on, to punish one person for what someone else has done.[13]

These three categories of moral values—the positive duties of mutual care and reciprocity; the negative injunctions concerning violence, deceit, and betrayal; and the norms for certain rudimentary procedures and standards for what is just—go into what P. F. Strawson has referred to as a "minimal interpretation of morality"— one that takes the recognition of certain virtues and obligations to be a "condition of the existence of a society": There are certain rules of conduct that any society must stress if it is to be viable. These

11. *Constructions of Reason: Explorations of Kant's Practical Philosophy* (Cambridge: Cambridge University Press, 1989), 215–18.

12. See Richard H. Underwood, "False Witness: A Lawyer's History of the Law of Perjury," *Arizona Journal of International and Comparative Law* 10 (1993): 215–52.

13. Arnold Brecht, *Political Theory* (Princeton: Princeton University Press, 1959), 389, 396. For a discussion of the development of concepts of fairness and morality in childhood, see Jean Piaget, *The Moral Judgment of the Child* (London: Kegan, Paul, Trench, Trubner and Co., 1932).

include "the abstract virtue of justice, some form of obligation to mutual aid and mutual abstention from injury, and, in some form and in some degree, the virtue of honesty."[14]

Because no society can do without at least rudimentary rules of this kind, they are recognized across all cultural and other boundaries. Injunctions such as those to honor one's parents or not to bear false witness, for example, are more readily recognized from one group to another than, say, claims about one or another religious dogma or moral theory or political system, and can therefore more easily be understood as shared. Thus those two injunctions, as stated in two of the Ten Commandments, resonate more universally than the Commandments to make no graven image and to hold the Sabbath day holy. Likewise, the injunctions to nonkilling, truthfulness, and nonstealing, which are part of the *Yama*, or first step of *Raja-Yoga*, receive more widespread assent than that of "non-receiving of any gift," which also forms part of that first step.[15] And those elements of the Buddhist Noble Eightfold Path that concern avoidance of false speech, the taking of life, and stealing are recognizable the world over in a way that is not true of those other elements that ask that one should abstain from making one's living through a profession, such as trading in arms, that brings harm to others.[16]

The fact that certain values are so widely recognized does not mean that people automatically acknowledge them as held in common, least of all among enemy groups. On the contrary, the tendency to regard outsiders and enemies as less than human, barbarians, utterly alien from a moral point of view, is well known. And the three categories of value are limited in scope even within communities. Violence, for example, against women, or children, or slaves and servants has been common from biblical times on.

In setting forth the three categories of values, therefore, my intention is not to suggest that they can somehow serve right away as

14. P. F. Strawson, "Social Morality and Individual Ideal," in G. Wallace and A. D. M. Walker, eds., *The Definition of Morality* (London: Methuen and Co., 1970), 101–3, 111.

15. Swami Vivekananda, *Raja-Yoga or Conquering the Internal Nature* (Mayavati, Almora, Himalayas: Advaita Ashrama, 1937), 21.

16. Walpola Sri Rahula, *What the Buddha Taught* (New York: Grove Press, 1974), 48.

cross-cultural standards of conduct. The difficulties of extending the perceived scope of these values within societies as well as among them are great. Rather, I suggest viewing them in a minimalist perspective. The term *minimalist* is increasingly used to characterize a limited set of fundamental values, helpful in specifying the characteristics and possible functions of values recognizable across cultural and other boundaries.[17] I suggest that these types of values are minimalist ones in at least the following senses:

• They are limited in number, in scope, and in degree of elaboration. They are therefore far from constituting entire systems of ethics, law, or theology and have arisen before any such systems were formally elaborated. They represent the bare bones of more abstract and complex values and ideals such as "love," "truth," "respect for life," "fidelity," "equality," "integrity," and "justice."

• Consequently, minimalist values require no special erudition, or even literacy, to be understood.

• They concern primarily what people should do or not do, rather than all that they may plan, fear, intend, dream of, or feel tempted by.

• They start out from clear-cut cases, as in the injunction not to kill, leaving open the question of how to evaluate borderline cases.

• They call for no agreement as to their source, foundation, or construction. People may differ in basing their view of lying, for example, on assumptions about divine authority, natural law, community agreement, moral sense, utilitarian reasons, or autonomous choice.

• They may not be the only values necessary for collective survival: indeed, certain other values such as a constraint on official secrecy have come to be stressed only in the past three centuries but are now increasingly seen as indispensable for public officials and others bound by rules of accountability.[18]

• No claim to universal acceptance need be made for these values: there will always be persons who reject every moral value including the most basic ones. But the amoralist, as Bernard Williams points

17. I draw on a number of contemporary thinkers in referring to minimalist values. See discussion and references in Chapter 2.

18. Sissela Bok, *Secrets: On the Ethics of Concealment and Revelation* (New York: Pantheon Books, 1982); *A Strategy for Peace,* chaps. 2 and 4.

out, is "a parasite on the moral system. . . . For, in general, there can be no society without some moral rules, and he needs society."[19] In addition, while the minimalist moral values have arisen in most societies, stressing their commonality does not call for proof that no group whatsoever has survived without them.

• Nor, finally, are such minimalist values absolute in that they allow for no exceptions. While *constraints* on lying and violence, for instance, are stressed in all traditions, more stringent total prohibitions of such conduct are not.

Given that minimalist moral values are so widely to be found, they offer a basis on which to build negotiation and dialogue about how to extend the scope within which they are honored.[20] In turn, they also provide criteria and a broadly comprehensible language for critique of existing practices. Within societies, they can shape a dialogue about why certain groups are left out of consideration when it comes to even the most fundamental forms of respect. Across societal boundaries, taking these values seriously can support claims that the constraint on murder, say, or child abuse or enslavement, should not be restricted to one's own society and that cross-cultural critique is fully justified with respect to such political or religious practices as torture or human sacrifice, as well as to political, theological, or moral theories that endorse such practices.

> **2. These basic values are indispensable to human coexistence, though far from sufficient, at every level of personal and working life and of family, community, national, and international relations.**

In all cultures, the socializing process involves fostering a recognition of shared cultural values in children. Central to these shared

---

19. *Morality: An Introduction to Ethics* (New York: Harper and Row, 1972), 4.

20. See Hans Jonas, *The Imperative of Responsibility: In Search of an Ethics for the Technological Age* (Chicago: University of Chicago Press, 1984), for a view of the need to stretch perspectives on values in the light of contemporary circumstances.

values are the minimalist ones to which I have referred.[21] But although it is thought necessary to develop a modicum of respect for such values in any family or group, doing so is hardly regarded as sufficient. From the very beginning of life, children are also surrounded by other values, more numerous, more richly developed, and intertwined in more complex ways. These values may be contrasted to the minimalist, bare-bones ones as being "maximalist." Particular sets of values may be more or less maximalist along all of the dimensions mentioned above for minimalist values:

• Maximalist moral values may be more numerous, extensive, and elaborated. They may approximate or constitute entire systems of ethics, law, or theology, and concern more abstract and complex values and ideals such as "love," "truth," "respect for life," "fidelity," "integrity," "equality," and "justice."

• Some among these values may require special erudition to be understood.

• They may concern not only what people should do or not do, but also what they may plan, fear, intend, dream of, or feel tempted by.

• They may include precepts or methods for how to evaluate conflicts and borderline cases.

• Holders of maximalist values may insist on agreement as to their source, foundation, or construction.

• They may insist, likewise, on more than minimalist values as necessary for collective survival.

• They may claim that such values are or must be universally accepted.

• Likewise, they may regard some such values as absolute in that they allow for no exceptions.

Given all the ways in which views about values vary along one or more of these dimensions, the richness and profusion of maximalist traditions should surprise no one, the less so as both minimalist and maximalist values may be held in conjunction with differing

---

21. See Strawson, "Social Morality," 113–18, for a discussion of how the minimal values characteristically form the basis for moral development, and can then "assume more refined and generous shapes."

aesthetic, religious, economic, and other values. All may be reflected in views about virtues and traits of character, and contrasted to vices or failures of character. Individual maximalist value structures, moreover, operate in conjunction with, sometimes in opposition to, maximalist values of particular cultures, professions, or other groupings. Thus the complex of traditions, histories, and particular practices in family lore or patriotic sentiments forms a maximalist web of values; so do legal systems, theologies, political and moral theories, as well as views about the correct standards for particular professions, stages of life, and levels of society.

While necessary, minimalist values are nowhere near sufficient for a good life, for being in full touch with one's humanity, for a thriving family or community. Rather, they represent the minimum of what we can ask of ourselves and of what we owe to others, but not in any way all that we might owe to, or ask of, those who stand in special relations to us, such as our family members, friends, colleagues, clients, or political representatives; nor all that we might aspire to in terms of the respect due to all human beings, ourselves included.

In debates about moral issues, minimalist and maximalist perspectives enrich one another, providing mutually challenging and reinforcing approaches. The minimalist approach seeks common ground, some baseline consensus from which to undertake and facilitate further debate. The maximalist approach begins, rather, by setting forth a more complete position—often an ideal position seen as the correct one, whether or not it is generally shared. It is when these approaches are seen as different, each necessary but neither one sufficient on its own, that they best serve debates concerning values.[22]

Whenever, in the complex interactions involving values, the minimalist values are undermined or overridden altogether, human

---

22. I have discussed the maximalist and minimalist approaches with respect to moral issues concerning population policy in "Population and Ethics: Expanding the Moral Space," in Gita Sen, Adrienne Germain, and Lincoln Chen, eds., *Population Policies Reconsidered: Health, Empowerment, and Rights* (Cambridge: Harvard Series on Population and International Health, 1994), 15–26.

relationships suffer. We see the results, for example, in families rent by domestic violence, in governments overwhelmed by corruption, or in societies decimated and disgraced by "ethnic cleansing." In addition to all the suffering wrought under such circumstances, what is lost is the basis for even minimal mutual trust, and in turn the possibility for good-faith negotiation and cooperation.

Philosophers and theologians have long pointed to the corrosive effects on trust of violations of fundamental moral standards. More recently, Kenneth Arrow, Partha Dasgupta, and other social scientists have studied the institutional costs of practices destructive of trust.[23] They have argued that trust can be seen as a public good, much as water and air, that can increase the efficiency of any system but that cannot easily be bought, and that can become depleted if not respected.

In *Lying: Moral Choice in Public and Private Life*, I wrote of trust as a social good to be promoted just as much as the air we breathe or the water we drink.[24] At the time the book appeared, in the wake of Watergate and the war in Vietnam, public trust in government had reached new lows. Yet those who had contributed to eroding this social good had rarely taken this damage into consideration as they engaged in the deceit and lawlessness that generated lasting distrust, not only in themselves but in all public officials.

I have pursued this view of trust as a social good in later works, through an analogy between the social atmosphere in which all human interaction takes place and our natural atmosphere.[25] Trust is the prime constituent of the social atmosphere. It is as urgent not to damage that atmosphere by contributing to the erosion of trust as it is to prevent and attempt to reverse damage to our natural atmosphere. Both forms of damage are cumulative; both are hard to

23. Arrow, *The Limits of Organization* (New York: Norton, 1974), chap. 4; Dasgupta, "Trust as a Commodity," in D. Gambetta, ed., *Trust: Making and Breaking Cooperative Relations* (Oxford: Blackwell, 1988), 49–72. See also Bok, *A Strategy for Peace*, chap. 2, and "Can Lawyers Be Trusted?" *University of Pennsylvania Law Review* 138 (January 1990): 913–33.

24. *Lying: Moral Choice in Public and Private Life* (New York: Pantheon Books, 1978), 26.

25. See Bok, *A Strategy for Peace*, introduction, and "Can Lawyers Be Trusted?," 919–20.

reverse. To be sure, a measure of distrust is indispensable in most human interaction. Pure trust is no more conducive to survival in the social environment than is pure oxygen in Earth's atmosphere. But too high a level of distrust stifles cooperation as much as the lack of oxygen threatens life.

Every human relationship, whether in families, on city blocks, in communities, in professional contexts, or in international relations, thrives only as long as a minimum of trust is maintained. When trust is damaged or decimated, through violence, dishonesty, betrayal, injustice, or the failure to nurture the young and those in need, these relationships suffer. It is infinitely harder to work at regaining trust, once it has been lost, than to squander it in the first place. And to the degree that trust is damaged or lost, dialogue and efforts at cooperation in the face of common threats are hobbled from the outset.

3. It is possible to affirm both common values and respect for diversity and in this way to use the basic values to critique abuses perpetrated in the name either of more general values or of ethnic, religious, political, or other diversity.

People in different cultures will never come to share any one of the complex religious and political traditions that have evolved over many centuries; and we shouldn't want this to happen. The uniqueness of so many different traditions enriches all of our cultural heritage, and cultural diversity may be as important as biological diversity for the purposes of survival and thriving.[26] We can strive to reach out to all cultures no matter how varied their practices and views, and learn from the various maximalist views that they embody; but in so doing, we need to consider, also, the degree to which they respect the fundamental minimalist values in practice.

These values provide, as suggested above, a common language in which to conduct a dialogue about what further agreement may

26. See Amélie Oksenberg Rorty, "The Advantages of Moral Diversity," *Social Philosophy and Policy* 9:2 (1992): 38–62.

be possible, and what disagreements remain. They also offer common standards for critiquing practices such as those of torture, or religious persecution, even when carried out in the name of purportedly higher religious or political values. To this day, every crime against humanity, including "ethnic cleansing" and genocide, is carried out under the banners of justice, liberty, religious zeal, or racial superiority. As Bernard Williams has pointed out, to the extent that we emphasize only "the local significances of a densely structured traditional existence," we have no point of leverage for criticism.[27] The same is true to the extent that we emphasize only abstract ideals, such as that of justice, without seeing their roots in the most basic, down-to-earth minimalist values needed for the survival of any community.

Cultural diversity can and should be honored, but only within the context of respect for common values. Any claim to diversity that violates minimalist values—such as claims defending child prostitution or the mutilation of girls and women on "cultural" or "aesthetic" grounds or insisting that human sacrifice is religiously mandated—can be critiqued on cross-cultural grounds invoking the basic respect due all human beings.

Such a critique does not advocate sameness or uniformity. It places no obstacles in the way of the most wide-ranging interests or the highest ideals, so long as the minimalist values are upheld. It assumes that individuals, professions in their codes of ethics, religious organizations, political parties, and other groups should be free to set for themselves the most diverse goals and aspirations, and the highest standards of conduct, so long as these don't violate the minimalist values. Health professionals, for example, can require particular skills, and enjoin respect for particular obligations to patients; but these ideals and obligations must not, as is too often the case, be used to defend lying to patients in what is thought, unreflectively, to be in their best interest, or in that of conducting scientific research.[28]

---

27. Bernard Williams, "Left-Wing Wittgenstein, Right-Wing Marx," *Common Knowledge* 1 (spring 1992): 37.

28. See Bok, *Lying,* for a discussion of lying in medicine and in other professional and personal contexts.

It is not the case, then, that "anything goes" so long as it is defended on moral or cultural or professional or religious grounds. Those who argue most vociferously to the contrary are usually defending their own right to violate moral standards as they see fit—not the individuals whose lives and security and self-respect they threaten. But apart from such violations, the richness of cultural and individual variation should be relished, not decried. As Claude Lévi-Strauss puts it, in speaking of the necessity of preserving the diversity of cultures in a world threatened by monotony and uniformity: "The diversity of human cultures is behind us, around us, and ahead of us. The only demand we may make upon it (creating for each individual corresponding duties) is that it realize itself in forms such that each is a contribution to the greater generosity of others."[29]

> *4. The need to pursue the inquiry about which basic values can be shared across cultural boundaries is urgent, if societies are to have some common ground for cross-cultural dialogue and for debate about how best to cope with military, environmental, and other hazards that, themselves, do not stop at such boundaries.*

A degree of adherence to minimalist values, rooted in the biological and social survival needs of families, groups, and larger communities, is what makes minimal trust, and therefore cooperation, possible. This need for values for purposes of group survival, whether considered from the point of view of families, tribes, communities, or nations, must now also be taken into account for purposes of collective survival. Societies face threats that respect no linguistic, ethnic, or other boundaries and that cannot be overcome on a piecemeal basis. Environmental deterioration; epidemics such as AIDS; the exhaustion of scarce resources; escalating numbers of

29. *Structural Anthropology* (1958; Chicago: University of Chicago Press, 1976), 2:362. See also Adam Kuper, *The Chosen Primate: Human Nature and Cultural Diversity* (Cambridge: Harvard University Press, 1994).

homeless persons and refugees; the possible doubling of Earth's population in the decades to come; the spread of "complex human- itarian emergencies" such as those in Bosnia, Rwanda, and so many other regions; the growing risk of nuclear proliferation; and threats to Earth's ozone layer are among the challenges that call most clearly for collective, cross-cultural responses.

If societies are to have some basis, some common ground, for dialogue about how best to respond to threats that so clearly call for cooperation at levels higher than ever mustered in the past, then the same values will have to be taken into account internationally that have long operated on a smaller scale. I have suggested beginning with a minimalist conception of three categories of fundamental val- ues: positive duties of care and reciprocity; constraints on violence, deceit, and betrayal; and norms for procedures and standards for what is just. Many past efforts to proselytize and conquer in the name of universal values have turned out to violate these mini- malist duties, constraints, and standards—above all, the constraint on violence. Without doing much more than in the past to work out a shared basis of values permitting genuine debate, dialogue, and critique, it is unrealistic to imagine that societies will muster adequate collective responses to these threats.

This effort must be two-pronged. It must operate both at the most down-to-earth level of seeking out and debating which are the basic, common values that can best serve the purposes of di- alogue and cooperation and at the level of abstract ideals such as "liberty," "equality," "democracy," or "human solidarity." Such ideals are important ones, but they cannot be easily and directly applied in the absence of careful consideration of such linkage.[30] They are often coarsely misused by all sides in even the bloodi- est of conflicts. What is needed, rather, is to sort out the linkage between such ideals and values that are common enough and spe- cific enough so that they can be applied, in the sense proposed by

30. For a discussion of the role and context of abstract values, see Martha Nussbaum, "Valuing Values: A Case of Reasoned Commitment," *Yale Journal of Law and the Humanities* 6:2 (summer 1994): 197–217.

Samuel Johnson: they must be capable of being "put to the use of life."[31]

Johnson points out,

> [I]n moral discussions it is to be remembered that many impediments obstruct our practice, which very easily give way to theory. The speculationtist is only in danger of erroneous reasoning, but the man involved in life has his own passions and those of others to encounter, and is embarrassed with a thousand inconveniences, which confound him with variety of impulse, and either perplex or obstruct his way. He is forced to act without deliberation, and obliged to choose before he can examine; he is surprised by sudden alterations of the state of things, and changes his measure according to superficial appearances; he is led by others, either because he is indolent or because he is timorous; he is sometimes afraid to know what is right, and sometimes finds friends or enemies diligent to deceive him.[32]

Debates about values that ignore such practical impediments only serve to increase the felt difference between rhetoric and reality that undercuts adequate responses to human problems. How, then, might we best keep those "impediments that obstruct our practice" in full view?

Most important, for this purpose, is simply to keep the practices themselves in view even as we debate the values that should guide them: to make every effort not to blind ourselves to the predicament of the human beings involved, not to give in to "compassion fatigue" or a flight into abstraction. In addition, it will help to move back and forth between several sets of perspectives so as to keep the tensions between them as clearly in mind as possible: to move between a minimalist perspective, seeking common ground in some baseline consensus, and differing maximalist perspectives, offering more completely elaborated positions; to move between the perspectives of practical ethics and those of moral theory in considering both the most down-to-earth practical injunctions and more abstract principles; and—perhaps hardest of all for many—to make every

31. *The Rambler* (1750; New York: Dutton, Everyman's Library, 1957), 31.
32. Ibid.

effort to move between perspectives on ethics based on secular and on religious convictions.

Debates concerning cross-cultural values in all these contexts are multiplying.[33] They are in part the result of challenges to the very idea that common values exist or that they are compatible with the fullest respect for diversity; but they reflect, too, the growing recognition of the need for a basis for more fruitful cooperative action. Four recent examples of efforts to seek out, propose, or explain moral standards so fundamental as to apply to the conduct of all individuals, groups, and societies bear witness to the scope of the resulting debates. Each of the four results from the intensive, often passionate deliberation and negotiation that serious efforts to address such issues must bring out. My purpose here is not to discuss the four in the detail that each one deserves, but rather to concentrate on the role of minimalist and maximalist approaches in each one. Two are religious in nature, two secular:

1. The United Nations World Conference on Human Rights, held in Vienna in June 1993.

2. The World Parliament of Religions, assembled in Chicago in August 1993.

3. *Veritatis Splendor,* Pope John Paul II's encyclical, published in the fall of 1993.

4. The Report of the Commission on Global Governance, *Our Global Neighborhood,* issued in February 1995.

---

33. See, for discussions of these issues, Zygmunt Bauman, *Postmodern Ethics* (Oxford: Blackwell, 1993); Tom L. Beauchamp and James F. Childress, *Principles of Medical Ethics,* 4th ed. (Oxford: Oxford University Press, 1994); William J. Bennett, *The Book of Virtues* (New York: Simon and Schuster, 1994); Richard B. Brandt, *Ethical Theory* (Englewood Cliffs, N.J.: Prentice Hall, 1959); Alan Donagan, *The Theory of Morality* (Chicago: University of Chicago Press, 1977); Richard Garner, *Beyond Morality* (Philadelphia: Temple University Press, 1994); Bernard Gert, *Morality: A New Justification of the Moral Rules* (Oxford: Oxford University Press, 1988); Alan Gewirth, *Reason and Morality* (Chicago: University of Chicago Press, 1978); Frances V. Harbour, "Basic Moral Values: A Shared Core," *Ethics and International Affairs* 9 (1995): 155–70; Martha Nussbaum, *The Fragility of Goodness: Luck and Ethics in Greek Tragedy and Philosophy* (Cambridge: Cambridge University Press, 1986); Gene Outka and John P. Reeder, Jr., eds., *Prospects for a Common Morality* (Princeton: Princeton University Press, 1993); Warnock, *Uses of Philosophy;* James Q. Wilson, *The Moral Sense* (New York: Free Press, 1993).

Four Approaches to Common Values

■   *1. The United Nations World Conference on Human Rights.*

At the June 1993 United Nations World Conference on Human Rights, thousands of participants from 183 nations convened in Vienna to seek agreement on a Declaration on Human Rights and a Program of Action. Never before had there been such diversity of nationalities and cultural traditions, dealing so outspokenly with questions of common values in the context of respect for diversity. And never before had the pervasive denial of rights to women in most societies been so forcefully shown to clash with the rhetoric about supposedly universal rights. On this and other scores, the conference brought into the open profound disagreements often concealed in the past beneath bland invocations of justice and human dignity.

The disagreements concerned what rights are due to individuals and what institutions should enforce such rights. If governments have this responsibility, what if these governments themselves are the prime violators of human rights, or have collapsed to the degree that they can offer no protection to victims? Exactly what does having a particular right entitle a person to? Are there group rights, and, if so, when do they override individual rights? What does a government's commitment to "promote" human rights commit it to in practice? What about rights violated, not by governments or public bodies, but by private individuals?

A coalition of Asian governments headed by delegates from China, Indonesia, and Malaysia argued for a trade-off between economic well-being and the full-scale political rights that they characterized as "Western notions." Others responded that access even to food and shelter can depend on being able to exercise political rights and that the notion that Asian cultures had no traditions of such rights was voiced by authoritarian regimes, not by the peoples currently deprived of the rights in question. Amartya Sen has pointed out that famines occur precisely in societies denying individual rights and lacking a free press, where the information needed to force government response to the crisis cannot be freely disseminated.[34]

The declaration affirms a universal and inalienable "right to development" while asserting that the central subject of development is the human individual, not groups or states, and that the lack of development "may not be invoked to justify the abridgement of internationally recognized human rights."[35] It would have been important to distinguish, here, between fundamental human rights and the entire list of rights that are "internationally recognized" only on paper. It is of crucial importance to speak out against states resorting to slave labor, torture, and the denial of political liberties in the name of "development." Every repressive government knows how to invoke development imperatives as a reason to override basic human rights. But even the least repressive societies weigh development needs against the promotion of certain entitlement rights such as that to "rest and leisure, including reasonable limitation of working hours and periodic holidays with pay."[36] So long as such balancing of priorities is subject to democratic procedures of approval or disapproval, it is not clear why it should be ruled out so peremptorily.

The failure to distinguish between the most basic human rights and all others leads to the uncritical claim, in clause 5 of the declaration, that "All human rights are universal, indivisible and interdependent and interrelated."[37] Interrelated? Indisputably. Interdependent? Truer of certain clusters of rights than of all. But indivisible? Hardly. Such confused, all-encompassing language makes it easy for critics to dismiss the entire list of rights as sheer rhetoric. Even the richest countries in the world, after all, cannot guarantee all the rights on that list, least of all if they are seen as indivisible.

34. See Kim Dae Jung, "Is Culture Destiny? The Myth of Asia's Anti-Democratic Values," *Foreign Affairs* (November/December 1994): 189–94; "Freedom and Needs," *New Republic,* January 10 and 17, 1994, pp. 31–38.
35. "Vienna Declaration of Human Rights," I.10, *Population and Development Review* 19:4 (December 1993): 878.
36. "Universal Declaration of Human Rights," United Nations, 1948, reaffirmed at Vienna in 1993, article 24.
37. "Vienna Declaration on Human Rights," I.5.

Jeremy Bentham's reference to talk of human rights as "rhetorical nonsense—nonsense upon stilts," however inappropriate with respect to many rights claims, surely applies here.[38]

The confusing language may represent efforts to paper over controversy. The discussion would have benefited from distinguishing between a minimalist and a maximalist approach: between seeking agreement on fundamental rights such as those not to be enslaved, tortured, killed, prevented from speaking out or from exercising one's religion, on the one hand, and, on the other hand, encouraging serious debate about aspirations we may share for all human beings, such as adequate educational opportunities, a guaranteed job, adequate vacation time, and developmental opportunities.[39]

■ *2. The World Parliament of Religions.*

A second collective effort to explore common values took place at the World Parliament of Religions, convened at Chicago at the end of August 1993, assembling religious leaders from around the world. This effort was much more explicitly governed by a minimalist perspective on the prospects for shared values in the context of the richest religious and cultural diversity. Yet it, too, ended by interspersing a number of maximalist claims among the minimalist ones, in the declaration entitled "Towards a Global Ethic," formulated by a subgroup of religious leaders at the parliament.

The document's subtitle is "An Initial Declaration," and readers are invited to take part in what is expressly stated to be "an initial effort: a point of beginning for a world sorely in need of consensus."[40] The declaration was written by Hans Küng, a Roman Catholic theologian, himself the author of a book setting forth an

38. "A Critical Examination of the Declaration of Rights," in Bhiku Parekh, ed., *Bentham's Political Thought* (London: Croom, Helm, 1973).

39. See John Rawls, "The Law of Peoples," in Stephen Shute and Susan Hurley, eds., *On Human Rights: The Oxford Amnesty Lectures 1993* (New York: Basic Books, 1993), 41–82, for such a distinction.

40. "Towards a Global Ethic," Council for a Parliament of the World's Religions, 1993, title page.

explicitly minimalist ethic as capable of being shared worldwide.[41] The aim was to formulate one underlying set of moral values that were already recognized in all religions, all cultures, and that could therefore be openly accepted by all, from all religious as well as secular moral traditions. On the basis of such a set of values, the declaration criticizes the violations of even the most basic rights by citizens and states in many parts of the world. It singles out for particular condemnation "aggression and hatred in the name of religion."[42] Such a statement can form the basis for a critique, from a minimalist moral perspective, of the vendettas, the persecutions, the holy wars, and the inquisitions still routinely perpetrated by many religious authorities.

The declaration sets forth an often admirable agenda for working toward greater tolerance, mutual trust, and cooperation, within communities as well as between them. But it does not carry out the announced intention of singling out a core of values acceptable to all. As a result, it sometimes conveys intolerance toward those not capable of living up to the highest maximalist ideals. Thus it sets forth the Golden Rule peremptorily as an "irrevocable, unconditional norm for all areas of life, for families and communities, for races, nations, and religions."[43] It is difficult to know what "irrevocable" and "unconditional" mean in this context, unless the reference is to divine lawmaking or to some other explicit laying down of the law or decreeing of a kind that would surely astonish those who, like Hillel or Confucius, first formulated the Rule.

The declaration goes on to interpret this Rule in an idiosyncratic, expansive, and far from universally accepted manner, as urging that "every form of egoism should be rejected: All forms of selfishness, whether individual or collective, whether in the form of class thinking, racism, nationalism, or sexism."[44] Asking for the rejection

---

41. *Global Responsibility: In Search of a New World Ethic* (New York: Crossroad Publishing Co., 1991). For a discussion of Küng's views in the context of other views on common values, see Rushworth M. Kidder, *How Good People Make Tough Choices* (New York: William Morrow and Co., 1995).

42. "Towards a Global Ethic," 1.

43. Ibid., 5.

44. Ibid.

of *all* forms of egoism or selfishness is to call for a level of self-abnegation possible for very few: a level, moreover, that again goes beyond the interpretation given to the Rule by Hillel, Confucius, or most other commentators. Having interpreted the Rule thus, the document proceeds to claim that it gives rise to four "broad, ancient guidelines for human behavior":

• Commitment to a culture of nonviolence and respect for life.
• Commitment to a culture of solidarity and a just economic order.
• Commitment to a culture of tolerance and a life of truthfulness.
• Commitment to a culture of equal rights and partnership between men and women.[45]

These guidelines are not held forth, however, even by most of the world's major religions, let alone many secular traditions. As a result, they cannot be thought of as minimalist, however desirable in their own right. True, certain minimalist values are emphasized at several points within the broad maximalist framework of these four commitments. The trouble is that the minimalist values are scattered among the maximalist ones without clear distinctions being drawn. Thus the first commitment refers not only to a constraint on violence but also of nonviolence and respect for all life, including that of animals and plants. The second commitment moves from stressing not stealing to a critique of materialism, calls for a just economic order, and a claim that "no one has the right to use his or her possessions without concern for the needs of society and Earth." The third commitment denounces lying but also enjoins living lives of truthfulness; and the fourth moves from condemning sexual immorality to rejecting "patriarchal domination and degradation."[46]

Given Dr. Küng's earlier express endorsement of a minimalist ethics, it is especially surprising that the declaration ended up going so far beyond minimalist claims without separating the two types of claims more clearly for purposes of debate. Perhaps most troubling from this point of view is the declaration's flamboyant call, at the

45. Ibid., 5–9.
46. Ibid., 7, 9.

end, for a global "transformation of consciousness!" Such a call is
not designed to enlist agreement among the more than 20 percent of
humanity estimated to be without religious allegiance, nor among
the many religious persons wary of such transformation.[47] At the
individual level, a transformation of consciousness may be sought
as a step toward spiritual advancement. Even then, it carries risks
whenever it bypasses reflection and moral judgment. But these risks
are magnified when the call goes out for a collective, let alone global,
transformation of consciousness.[48] At the very least, the authors
should have acknowledged that the desire for such transformation
is neither common to all traditions nor necessary for the purposes
of working for common goals.

■ 3. Veritatis Splendor, *Pope John Paul II's encyclical.*

Pope John Paul II takes a different approach to the question of
common values in his 1993 encyclical *Veritatis Splendor* (*The Splendor
of Truth*). He makes clear from the outset that he intends to present
a fully worked out maximalist system of absolutely binding values
meant for all of humankind, in response to the fundamental questions shared by all, no matter how diverse their backgrounds: "What
must I do? How do I distinguish good from evil?"[49] But while the
encyclical, like the Vienna Human Rights Declaration and "Towards
a Global Ethic," endorses an unequivocally maximalist set of values,

47. "If our world were a village of 1000 people, there would be 329 Christians,
174 Muslims, 131 Hindus, 61 Buddhists, 52 Animists, 3 Jews, 34 members of other
religions, 216 without any religion" (World Development Forum, 1992, *Encyclopedia
Britannica Book of the Year*).

48. Had secular representatives taken part in preparing the declaration, they
might also have challenged as incomplete the claim that the common set of core
values capable of providing a basis for a global ethic is to be found in the teachings
of the world's religions; why not add that these values are also to be found in secular
texts and have been expressed before the world's religions were even formulated?
In the age-old debate as to whether something is right because God declares it
right or whether God declares it to be right because it can be shown to be right
on other grounds, it matters not to come down squarely on one side without at least
acknowledging the existence of the other.

49. Pope John Paul II, *Veritatis Splendor, Origins*, 23, October 14, 1993, p. 299.

the Pope has no intention, unlike the authors of these declarations, to present a document that is open to change at a later time. He is not inviting the criticism of those who disagree with him. Dissent, on the contrary, is ruled out, as is disobedience to the precepts taught by the Church. These "oblige everyone, regardless of the cost."[50]

The encyclical differs from the two declarations, moreover, in that it distinguishes between common values known everywhere and a system combining theological and moral propositions, showing the steps between them so clearly that readers have the opportunity to decide exactly where they can and cannot agree, and on what grounds. It refers to the parable (Matthew 19:16–21) in which a rich young man approaches Jesus to ask him what good he must do to have an eternal life. Jesus answers that there is only one who is good, then enjoins the young man to keep five commandments that fairly qualify as minimalist moral requirements: "You shall not murder; you shall not commit adultery; you shall not steal; you shall not bear false witness; honor your father and mother."[51] These precepts are known in most other traditions as well as being a part of the Judeo-Christian heritage, although, to be sure, they have always given rise to a variety of interpretations.

When the rich young man says that he has kept all these commandments and asks what he still lacks, Jesus answers: "If you wish to be perfect, go, sell your possessions and give money to the poor, and you will have treasure in heaven; then come, follow me." The encyclical makes it clear that the latter is indeed a maximalist requirement, whereas the five Commandments are a starting point, a foundation, for moral conduct. They constitute the "indispensable rules of all social life."[52] Had the young man been an unrepenting liar and thief, it would not have helped him to give away all he owned to follow Jesus.

---

50. Ibid., 313; see also 329–30.
51. Ibid., 300. Jesus adds, "also, you shall love your neighbor as yourself": a statement which, depending on how "love" and "neighbor" are interpreted, can be given either a minimalist or a maximalist meaning.
52. Ibid., 325.

But the encyclical goes on to argue that in each of the five Commandments mentioned, one can discern larger, more demanding positive duties: "the ever urgent need to protect human life, the communion of persons in marriage, private property, truthfulness, and people's good name." Ultimately, the commandments shed light on "the fundamental rights inherent in the nature of the human person" and "the basic condition for love of neighbor."[53] Pope John Paul II holds that the prohibitions of slavery, torture, genocide, and many other violations of the human person contained in the Declaration of Human Rights can be seen as following from these Commandments.

This is a minimalist claim that many could find persuasive, regardless of religious or political background. The same cannot be said for the further claim that contraceptive practices are evil because they are means of intentionally rendering the conjugal act infertile.[54] On this issue, the Pope differs greatly with many outside and inside the Roman Catholic Church. He can hardly derive the prohibition of contraception directly from the commandment not to engage in adultery nor from any of the other four on which he has relied. Rather, he supports it indirectly with inferences from biblical and other texts and with arguments invoking his and the Church's authority.

These arguments, along with those concerning the prohibitions of homosexuality and abortion, are maximalist, not only in that they go beyond principles commonly recognized everywhere, but also because they, like all the claims throughout the encyclical, are based on the premise that there is one and only one path to salvation, one and only one conception of what is right and what is wrong, one and only one foundation for all of morality in Christ, and one and only one legitimate interpretation of that morality, in the Church; and that, moreover, there can be no exceptions whatsoever to the moral rules and prohibition enunciated by the proper Church authorities.

Similarly absolutist claims are made by other religious and political leaders to support different sets of maximalist principles.

53. Ibid., 302.
54. Ibid., 321.

Outsiders to such traditions should not set such claims aside merely because the various claims clash with one another or because of their absolutist cast. Rather, it is important, in the international debates over values now under way, to examine the reasoning underlying each of the claims, seeking out what can and cannot help to elucidate these debates, even though the claims themselves are set forth as being, precisely, not open to debate.

▍ 4. *The Report of the Commission on Global Governance,* **Our Global Neighborhood.**

My final example of a statement of common values is that of the Commission on Global Governance, chaired by Sir Shridath Rampal, former foreign minister of Guyana and head of the British Commonwealth, and Ingvar Carlsson, prime minister of Sweden. In *Our Global Neighborhood,* the commission goes beyond previous reports and declarations, including the three discussed above, in providing factual documentation and careful discussion of the human realities that underlie the need for unprecedented levels of transnational cooperation.[55] It posits an unavoidable challenge for societies: they must learn to work together before it is too late, by transforming the present unruly, conflicted world neighborhood of peoples into a cooperating network of communities. To this purpose, some set of common values is indispensable. Rather than listing a large number of rights and pronouncing them indivisible, in the manner of the 1993 World Conference on Human Rights, the commission suggests a threefold approach: a basis of core values, a limited set of rights and responsibilities constituting a "civic code" that builds upon these, and changes in international norms embodying these values.

The three parts, thus ordered, might be thought to correspond with a movement from the most common, minimalist values to ones more recently seen as needed; but this is not the case. The list of core values that "all humanity could uphold" turns out to

55. The Commission on Global Governance, *Our Global Neighborhood* (Oxford: Oxford University Press, 1995), chap. 1.

consist of abstract moral principles such as respect for life, liberty, justice, and equity, mutual respect, caring, and integrity. Whether or not all humanity ever could uphold all of these principles together, it assuredly has not done so up to now. Take liberty, or freedom: as Orlando Patterson points out, "For most of human history, and for nearly all the non-Western world prior to Western contact, freedom was, and for many still remains, anything but an obvious or desirable goal."[56] Nor can "mutual respect," which the commission claims is "the more active attribute" of tolerance, be thought a fundamental value in communities or families from earliest times, any more than can "[r]espect for life and its corollary, non-violence," "integrity," or "justice and equity." Only minimalist forms of these values, such as the constraints on violence and deceit, and basic norms of procedural justice or fairness, are capable of being acknowledged by most people, at least with respect to their own community.

The commission vacillates, with respect to its list of core values, between unsupported empirical claims that peoples everywhere uphold one or another value, such as "the sanctity of life," and prescriptive claims that they must do so if we are to achieve peace and progress. Even if we disregard the empirical claims, the prescriptive ones give pause. Either we take the commission's core values as abstractions so vast and so toothless as to be capable of encompassing almost any practices, in which case they will be useless for the purposes of providing a ground for moving toward the goals set forth, of peace and progress; or else, if we try to give them more substance, more bite, then we can no longer see them as likely to be shared by "all humanity." In neither case can they serve as indispensable preconditions to the achievement of peace and progress. They turn out to ask either too little or too much for such a purpose.

What if we ask, not about present acceptance of the commission's core values, but rather about making stronger efforts to uphold them? Even so, it would be important to offer justifications for why

56. *Freedom*, vol. 1: *Freedom in the Making of Western Culture* (New York: Basic Books, 1991), x.

we ought to strive to uphold and extend the reach of these values. These justifications would have to refer to some more fundamental moral grounds that could be broadly accepted. In addition, the core values themselves are so vague that it would be difficult to know just how one might apply them, above all in cases of moral conflict. What does it mean to uphold or extend integrity? And how do we resolve disagreement among persons with differing views about what counts as integrity?

Most of the "rights and responsibilities" that the commission goes on to list as expressing the core values are equally general. This time, however, there is never any doubt as to their aspirational nature. True, the list is held to be "the minimum basis for progress in building a more civil global society."[57] But the rights and responsibilities in question are explicitly uniformly prescriptive. The global ethic of common rights and shared responsibilities

> *should* [emphasis added] encompass the rights of all people to: the rights to a secure life, equitable treatment, an opportunity to earn a fair living and provide for their own welfare, the definition and specification of their differences through peaceful means, participation in governance at all levels, free and fair petition for redress of gross injustices, equal access to information, and equal access to the global commons.
>
> At the same time, all people share a responsibility to: contribute to the common good; consider the impact of their actions on the security and welfare of others; promote equity, including gender equity; protect the interests of future generations by pursuing sustainable development and safeguarding the global commons; preserve humanity's cultural and intellectual heritage; be active in governance; and work to eliminate corruption.[58]

In this list of rights and responsibilities, as in that of the core values on which it is held to draw, the language is abstract and extremely general. The intention may have been to seek the broadest possible support. Who can quarrel, after all, with injunctions to contribute to the common good or to work to eliminate corruption?

---

57. *Global Neighborhood*, 57.
58. Ibid.

But anyone asking what, exactly, is meant by the various rights and responsibilities and how they relate to one another may wish to have some answers before subscribing to the entire list. What is meant, for instance, by the right of all people to provide for their own welfare? Or by the right of access to the global commons? And how do these rights relate to everyone's responsibility to protect the interests of future generations? The question, in general, of who should be held responsible for the provision of all these rights is perplexing. Do we have greater responsibilities toward our own children, family members, fellow citizens, than to others, in disposing of scarce resources? What sacrifices do our responsibilities to future generations call for? And how should the vast costs of implementing rights such as that of equal access to information be distributed?

Such questions about the substance and extent of rights and responsibilities underlie controversies between liberals and conservatives, between North and South, between ethnic and religious adversaries. For growing numbers of people, they are questions bearing on the survival of their ways of life, their communities, their descendants. The commission has itself pointed to the unprecedented levels of human need that necessitate seeking out a basis of common values on which debate and cooperation can be built.[59] But merely listing rights and responsibilities that are so general and so far from being commonly acknowledged cannot offer such a basis.

The commission's stress on the need for common values, like that of the other three documents discussed above, provides a partial answer to Herbert Schneider's question, quoted above, about how we might "formulate an ethics or a method of moral science which would serve the cause of morals for all mankind." All four efforts seek to formulate such an ethics to serve such a cause. In so doing, they take their departure from different perspectives and arrive at sometimes sharply different conclusions. But they also overlap

59. See, for critiques of the most general claims about human rights and corresponding responsibilities, O'Neill, *Constructions of Reason*, 187–205; Rawls, "The Law of Peoples," in Shute and Hurley, eds., *On Human Rights*, and other chapters in this volume; Amartya Sen, "Freedom and Needs."

when it comes to fundamental values. Among these are the three categories of values that I have suggested are minimalist values most easily recognized across societal and other boundaries: the most basic forms of the positive duties of care and reciprocity; of constraints on violence, deceit, and betrayal; and of norms for procedures and standards of justice.

The four approaches differ when it comes to aspirations, ideals, and principles of what I have called a maximalist nature. Looking at the four together helps to demonstrate how the maximalist and minimalist perspectives can challenge and enrich one another, how both are needed to push the debate still further, how such a debate can affirm both common values and respect for diversity, yet how distant the goal remains of a fully worked out and widely acknowledged common morality. The four texts, taken together, exemplify the importance increasingly attached to stressing common values, but also the questions of line-drawing and the theoretical and practical objections that any search for such values is bound to elicit. I turn to these issues in the chapters to come, beginning with strong contemporary challenges to the very premises on which such a search is based.

Chapter 2

The Search for a
Common Ethics

The thought of searching for an ethics capable of cutting across cultural boundaries strikes many contemporaries as either offensive or ludicrously naive. It seems offensive or at the very least redundant to all who see no need to search for values already self-evidently present since time immemorial or divinely revealed; and correspondingly naive to the many—often intellectuals—convinced that such a search is bound to fail. The skepticism of the latter is of ancient lineage; but it has been reinforced in our century by growing awareness of the uniqueness and diversity of cultures and of the crippling ethnocentrism of past efforts to subdue and convert and "civilize" in the name of values arrogantly labeled "universal."

It is understandable, in this context, that many should question the premises underlying efforts to seek out even a minimalist set of common values. Their doubts concern not so much the view that the need is urgent for such values to facilitate cross-cultural dialogue and cooperation, but rather the belief that a search for such values can possibly succeed. These doubts represent the most forceful contemporary obstacle to pursuing the inquiry into such values and, in turn, to exploring their role as a basis for collective efforts to serve common purposes. It matters, therefore, to examine the evidence and the reasoning on which the doubts are themselves based. We can no longer afford not to press the long-standing dialectic regarding "universal values" beyond today's conventional certainties about the self-evidence or nonexistence of such values.

Julien Benda's Prediction

> *Our century will truly have been the century of the intellectual*
> *organization of hatred. That will be one of its great claims to fame*
> *in the moral history of humanity.*
>
> Julien Benda, *La Trahison des clercs*[1]

The betrayal of which Benda accused his fellow intellectuals was that of deserting their traditional function of upholding the universal values of justice, truth, reason, and humanity, and instead engaging in parochial political infighting. For two thousand years, he asserted, intellectuals had served these values in their role as clerics in the "universal Church of the human spirit."[2] Even those who, like Spinoza or Zola, had joined battle in particular political causes, had done so in the name of those same universal values. But by the turn of the century, Benda argued, many among the world's foremost thinkers had come to betray their function by endorsing the parochial passions and degrading hatreds of race, class, party, and nation.[3]

The poisoning of the cultural climate that had resulted was the more pernicious, Benda argued, because of the seductive new theories these intellectuals had generated to extol violence in such causes. He pointed to a gulf, in this regard, separating the teachings of Socrates, Aquinas, Erasmus, Kant, Goethe, and other past thinkers from those of inflammatory modern writers such as Nietzsche, Sorel, Maurras, Kipling, and D'Annunzio. And he excoriated his many fellow intellectuals who were propagating the ideologies of militant nationalism, bolshevism, fascism, and national socialism.[4]

---

1. *La Trahison des clercs* (The betrayal of intellectuals) (Paris: Bernard Grasset, 1927), translated by Richard Aldington as *The Betrayal of the Intellectuals* (Boston: Beacon Press, 1955), 26. My translation.

2. *Trahison*, 54, 64. See also the appendix on "clerical values" in the 1946 French reissue.

3. Benda's list of debilitating passions omits his own vehemence against women, whom he saw as incapable of truly rational thinking and as the embodiment of the passion and irrationalism that he opposed.

4. For Benda's later views on these movements, see R. Nichols, *Treason, Tradition, and the Intellectual: Julien Benda and Political Discourse* (Lawrence: University Press of

Benda's verdict on our century stands: even more than he could have known in 1927, we have witnessed vast and shamelessly organized hatreds. His critique of the intellectuals whose work provided the theoretical foundations for these hatreds also holds; but his call for them to serve, instead, such universal values as justice, truth, reason, and humanity rings hollow to many today. They may agree with Richard Rorty that "The nature of truth is an unprofitable topic," the more so as the decades since Benda wrote have brought mounting evidence of deep-seated differences among cultures.[5] It has become harder than ever to fathom how "truth" and "justice" could have anything like the same meaning the world over—say, to a New Guinea headhunter and a computer programmer in Silicon Valley, or to militant enemy groups in the Middle East, the Indian subcontinent, the Balkans, or Africa. Or, for that matter, to fellow North Americans irrevocably split over issues such as those of abortion or capital punishment.

Even "reason," long held to be the defining characteristic of the human species, is now often seen as so differently manifested in different cultures as to render vacuous any substantive claims to universality. It is hardly surprising, therefore, that many have come to view the "humanity" for which Benda postulated a common moral history as a mere abstraction, and to envisage that history, in turn, as a congeries of narratives no single one of which need be regarded as more valid than the others. As Clifford Geertz puts it: "Caught up in some of the more shaking originalities of the twentieth century, the study of society seems on the way to becoming seriously irregular."[6]

Skepticism regarding the universality of each of the values Benda invoked now permeates not only history but fields as diverse as biology, anthropology, philosophy, and literary theory. And this skepticism has generated an interdisciplinary uniformity of language all

Kansas, 1978), and Jean Sarochi, *Julien Benda: Portrait d'un intellectuel* (Paris: A. G. Nizet, 1968).

5. Richard Rorty, *Contingency, Irony, and Solidarity* (New York: Cambridge University Press, 1989), 8.

6. Clifford Geertz, *Local Knowledge* (New York: Basic Books, 1983), 4.

its own. Scholars in these varied fields now speak in interchangeable terms, deploying metaphors of fragmentation, divergence, unmooring, and asymmetry to convey the thorough incommensurability of the values held in different cultural and linguistic communities.

Such metaphors have helped force a fresh look at the realities underlying long-held intuitions about eternal values and unchangeable human nature. But when these metaphors are applied indiscriminately, they risk congealing inquiry as solidly as do the dogmas they were meant to shatter. New certainties, as little examined as past ones, take hold. They permit new leaps of faith: from denying any divine purpose for humanity (or from noting irreconcilable disagreements regarding such a divine purpose) to asserting that human beings can share no purpose whatsoever; and from observing that any moral claim can be denied to concluding that no one moral stance is more valid than any other.

To the extent that you take such assertions seriously, they are bound to influence your ability to exercise practical moral judgment and in turn your decisions. For if you genuinely believe that other cultures are unknowable and that languages are mutually "untranslatable," then how can you venture to compare degrees of injustice, of oppression, of disrespect for fundamental human rights among societies? Or among subcultures in your own society? Or even from one individual to another?

For intellectuals who lock themselves into such reasoning, the options for principled practical choice shrink. Once again caught in the bewitchment by means of language of which Wittgenstein famously warned, they can then stare at, without seeing, the problems that now so clearly confront cultures collectively; and end by responding to these problems, if at all, with but a sense of wan impotence. In the perennial dialectic regarding shared human values, the temptation to rest satisfied with such passivity is as common as its converse— that of giving free rein to missionary zeal in furthering particular religious or political ideals seen as self-evident and bound to triumph. But whereas these temptations are hardly new, any more than the dialectic itself, they now pose a greater threat to the common good than ever. At the end of the century for which Benda predicted such a unique role, human societies have come to confront unprecedented and massive threats that even he could not have foreseen in 1927. There were then fewer than 2 billion people in the world; by now, that many are living at or near starvation levels and the world's population has tripled. The threats to Earth's atmosphere, its forests and farmlands, its oceans and waterways, and its cities transcend all cultural or linguistic boundaries.

As the international community begins to mobilize against these global dangers, the calls are mounting for efforts to combat human rights violations more vigorously than in the past. The Helsinki Accord in 1975 broke new ground in this respect: in elevating human rights to the same status as state rights, it provided a legal basis for human rights activism, citizen resistance, and international pressure, which contributed to the overthrow of the East European regimes in 1989, to the lifting of apartheid in South Africa, and to democracy movements in many parts of the world.[7] At the same time, however, egregious human rights violations in Bosnia, Rwanda, and so many other regions continue unabated. Human rights advocates are finding that it is one thing to focus on violations committed by governments against their own citizens and quite another to deal with atrocities committed on several sides in the humanitarian emergencies that have wrought such devastation since the end of the Cold War.[8]

Witnessing the contrast between the growing number of persons living in societies in which human rights struggles have borne fruit and that of the state of the victims denied every such right makes it necessary to amend Benda's views about our century's claim to fame. His prediction that it would be marked by the intellectual organization of hatred has been borne out in ways no one could have fully imagined in the 1920s; but this century has also been marked by an unprecedented mobilization of countervailing forces that Benda

7. For an account of the history of the human rights debate in our century, see Dorothy V. Jones, *Code of Peace: Ethics and Security in the World of the Warlord States* (Chicago: University of Chicago Press, 1989), 160. For responses to the contemporary human rights crises, see Stephen Shute and Susan Hurley, eds., *On Human Rights: The Oxford Amnesty Lectures 1993* (New York: Basic Books, 1993).

8. See Ian Martin, "The New World Order: Opportunity or Threat for Human Rights?" lecture, April 14, 1993, Harvard Law School Human Rights Program.

did not foresee: forces pressing for nonviolent social reform, the respect for human rights, and the peaceful resolution of conflict. Even as our century has witnessed the growth of ideologies perhaps as blatantly amoral as any in the past, so philosophies of nonviolent action such as those espoused by Mohandas Gandhi and Martin Luther King have challenged the unthinking recourse to force, and often succeeded in bringing about liberation and social change by other means.

Intellectuals have played an indispensable role in formulating, criticizing, and energizing the political struggles for freedom in societies the world over. Likewise, there is no dearth of inquiry and debate on the part of intellectuals regarding the political, economic, and scientific aspects of global problems. But discussions of the underlying moral questions cutting across cultural boundaries— when not ruled out of order altogether—are too often vacuous in the extreme. As Byron said in reading K. W. F. Schlegel, there is nothing to be taken hold of: "he always seems upon the verge of meaning; and lo, he goes down like a sunset, or melts like the rainbow, leaving a rather rich confusion."[9]

Such a meltdown is especially striking among those scientists who speak most forcefully about the urgency of how to respond to our collective predicament. Thus Albert Einstein, who did more than any individual in our century to open the public's eyes to the need for acknowledging the risks to humanity from "the release of atomic energy," called for something as improbable (and, if it arrived, as unaccountable) as a new way of thinking, and claimed that "old diplomatic conventions and balance of power politics ha[d] become utterly meaningless."[10] Jacques Monod, arguing that

9. George G. Byron, writing of Schlegel's *History of Literature* (Edinburgh, 1818) in *Letters and Journals* (Cambridge: Harvard University Press, 1978), 8:38.

10. Otto Nathan and Heinz Norden, *Einstein on Peace* (New York: Schocken Books, 1960), 407. Amartya Sen, in a comment on my reference to Einstein's call for a new way of thinking in the original article on which this chapter is based, argues persuasively that "The interdependence of human lives in the contemporary world and some recent examples of collaboration across the frontiers in such fields as environmental protection . . . surely point to the case for and the possibility of some departures from old ways of thinking" (Amartya Sen, "Three Questions," *Common Knowledge* 1 [winter 1992]: 25). I fully agree with Sen; but such categorical dismissals as those offered by

societies will collapse unless they define and adhere to a radically new value system, urged an austere but unspecified new "ethic of knowledge" as "the measure and warrant of all other values."[11] And the moral rhetoric concerning obligations and duties to Earth, the environment, and future generations that was marshaled in connection with the June 1992 Earth Summit in Rio de Janeiro was equally vacuous—the more glaringly so when compared to the substantive scientific and economic analyses of the growing threats to Earth's environment generated for the same conference. Such diffuse moral pronouncements cry out for the same critical analysis that scientists would be the first to require for strictly scientific hypotheses.

Critical analysis of the possibility, extent, and claimed justification of shared values has traditionally been thought to belong in the domain of humanists. If "the moral history of humanity" is now more and differently challenged than when Benda issued his cry of betrayal, then intellectuals—and foremost among them those humanists whose words carry weight in the intellectual world—have reason to reconsider their own role in facilitating or undermining the collective response now so clearly needed. In so doing, they can draw, as did their predecessors in the 1960s and 1970s, on the most recent available research. Thinkers in many disciplines are now challenging the skeptical orthodoxies of those decades. Evolutionary scientists, neurologists, and social scientists are exploring human commonalities. Philosophers, likewise, are questioning the doctrine of "untranslatability" among cultures, as are anthropologists.

An example of this questioning is provided by a new three-volume compendium in the Pléiade Library, entitled *Histoire des moeurs*. It aims to draw together current research and reflection from sources the world over regarding the richness and variability

---

Einstein of old ways of thinking, including old forms of political deliberation, offer further grist for the mill of the many who are already predisposed to opt out of all political processes unless or until some hoped-for transformation in thinking has taken place. The rejection of old ways of thinking then becomes one more delaying tactic, one more way to acknowledge in the abstract the dangers to which Einstein referred, while continuing to ignore them in practice.

11. *Chance and Necessity* (New York: Alfred A. Knopf, 1971), 176–80.

of social and cultural practices against a background of all that human beings and societies have in common: to analyze social and cultural practices, conduct intercultural comparisons, and delineate thematic syntheses concerning, for example, conduct relating to perceptions of time and space, nourishment, sexuality, the use of symbols, and morality. Jean Poirier, the editor and organizer of this collaborative undertaking, repeatedly stresses that an exhaustive inventory will always remain impossible and that there is much that can never be fully known about human beings; but he warns against pressing the notion of the unknowability of the "other" to the point of fetishism, which would amount to locking oneself into "a veritable cultural ghetto."[12]

Such warnings enjoin us to take seriously the doubts raised against overly simplistic past rhetoric about human nature and universal values, but without relying so uncritically on these doubts as to reject all study of what human beings have in common. This double caution is indispensable, I suggest, for anyone wishing to pursue the inquiry into common human values without slipping into premature closure—without either holding one particular set of values to be so self-evident as to require no further justification or allowing the rhetoric of moral incommensurability to block every inquiry concerning them. Merely to rehearse ingrained convictions about the meaning or meaninglessness of talk about universal values could otherwise come to constitute yet another *trahison des clercs*—albeit this time in postmodernist guise.

Survival Values

The preliminary first step, then, of an inquiry concerning common values is to bracket the conventional declarations supporting and denying the universality of values. Having done so, we can ask: Can

---

12. Jean Poirier, ed., *Histoire des moeurs* (Paris: Editions Gallimard, La Pléiade, 1990), 1399. For recent philosophical discussions of questions of intercultural communication and understanding, see the articles in Barry Smith and Tadashi Ogawa, eds., *Cultural Universals, The Monist* 78 (January 1995).

any values be said to be widely shared, and if so which ones? What obstacles stand in the way of perceiving them as widely held? And to what extent might at least some be acknowledged as requiring cross-cultural observance?

To seek answers to these questions, we need a starting point acceptable even to holders of widely different political, religious, and moral doctrines. One minimally controversial starting point is that of the biological survival needs that human beings share with a number of other species: the needs for at least enough nourishment, oxygen, water, and shelter not to perish. Infants everywhere need these to survive, even as they need warmth, human contact, and nurturing to thrive. Families and communities have to make provisions for these needs in order to ensure longer-term survival and thriving, and in turn for certain basic norms such as a constraint on killing, without which no group can survive. As H. L. A. Hart argues, reflection on some very obvious generalizations about human nature and the world in which people live shows that "as long as these hold good, there are certain rules of conduct which any social organization must contain if it is to be viable."[13]

Religious, legal, and moral traditions all stress a few basic duties and prohibitions such as those that Hart singles out as forming "the minimum content of Natural law."[14] All such traditions have further taken into account the degree to which human survival and thriving are affected both by external difficulties in securing adequate nourishment and shelter and also by threats of human origin. Stuart Hampshire has spoken of the experience of vulnerability to these two kinds of interlocking perils as common to all societies: "There is nothing mysterious or 'subjective' in the great evils of human experience, reaffirmed in every age and in every written history and in every tragedy and fiction: murder and destruction of life, imprisonment, enslavement, starvation, poverty, physical pain and torture, homelessness and friendlessness."[15]

13. *The Concept of Law* (Oxford: Clarendon Press, 1961), 186.
14. Ibid., 187.
15. *Innocence and Experience* (Cambridge: Harvard University Press, 1989), 90.

The widely experienced desire to guard against these evils provides a common perspective from which to reconsider the debate regarding shared values. Recent discussions by Hampshire and others of what might constitute a "minimalist ethics" offer a way to resume that debate.[16] Asking about common values in such a context requires searching, to begin with, not for entire systems of values that might be fully shared, but for a minimal set of values common to most communities; and it calls for concentrating, in that process, not immediately on the intricacies and ramifications of the most complex and abstract social values such as those of justice, truth, reason, and humanity, but rather on the constraints and practices worked out to guard against the most brutal injustices, the most debilitating untruths, and the most dangerous forms of unreason and inhumanity.

Although we may never achieve or know how to delimit complete justice, any more than absolute truth, perfect reason, or the fullest humanity, we have every reason to seek agreement as to what constitutes the most egregious departures from these ideals. Yet as Judith Shklar has argued with respect to injustice, these departures from our ideals have been far less thoroughly explored in philosophy and political theory than have the ideals themselves.[17]

To be sure, unanimity is out of the question, either about the justification for values seen as shared cross-culturally or about their being shared in the first place. There will always be individuals, alone or in groups, who reject commonly held values altogether or who differ about the content or scope of one or more of them. But unanimity is hardly needed for such an inquiry to begin. Nor

16. Such inquiries have long antecedents. See Chapters 1 and 4 in this book. Among contemporary works taking up such issues, see Hampshire, *Innocence and Experience;* Jones, *Code of Peace;* Hans Küng, *Projekt Weltethos* (Munich: Piper, 1990); Mary Maxwell, *Morality among Nations: An Evolutionary View* (Albany: State University of New York Press, 1990); Martha Nussbaum, "Aristotelian Social Democracy," in R. B. Douglass et al., *Liberation and the Good* (New York: Routledge, 1990); Thomas Pogge, *Realizing Rawls* (Ithaca: Cornell University Press, 1989), 219–28; Michael Walzer, "Moral Minimalism," in William R. Shea and Antonio Spadafora, eds., *From the Twilight of Probability: Ethics and Politics* (Canton, Mass.: Science History Publications, 1992).

17. *The Faces of Injustice* (New Haven: Yale University Press, 1990).

is confidence that such an inquiry will achieve significant practical results. Many continue to doubt the practical usefulness of inquiring into common values, given the severity of current ethnic and religious conflicts aflame or smoldering in many parts of the globe. This practically grounded skepticism is understandable; but it would be self-defeating to refuse even to entertain the possibility of a starting point that is based on shared concern for survival.

Once such a starting point is postulated, the search for a minimalist common ethics can proceed to sort out the common moral constraints and injunctions across communities and to pare down each one from the point of view of completeness, scope, and level of abstraction. It then becomes possible to ask to what extent the values thus singled out and pared down can offer more specific guidance than the more general ones invoked by Benda and others.

While a minimalist ethics offers a starting point and a rudimentary procedure for the pursuit of common goals, we have to recognize from the outset that it is far from sufficient. Without some version of such a minimalist ethics—one that includes basic forms of mutual support and procedural fairness and that prescribes curbs on intragroup harm—not even the smallest community can survive; but far more is needed for a family, a community, or a society to thrive. For that purpose, a richer, more complete "maximalist" ethics is required, as suggested in Chapter 1. Yet however insufficient a minimalist view of values may be for an adequate or flourishing human existence, much less an entire social structure, it is indispensable for cross-cultural cooperation. At the same time, it provides grounds for more comprehensive, "maximalist" views, however different in nature, as well as a common language in which to debate and evaluate the more complex questions these maximalist views raise.

This view of grounds is itself minimalist. It rejects the maximalist requirement that we achieve agreement concerning grounds that go "all the way down," or that are based on some one religious or moral or metaphysical doctrine, before relying on common values to facilitate cooperative measures. (See Chapter 3.) Rather, it postulates a minimal substratum of such values as offering grounds in other senses of that word: not only as a socially fashioned basis or foundation, but also as a set of reasons for a judgment, an action, a way of proceeding; and as itself rooted in shared human experience.

Minimalist Values

"Ah, you're a Maximalist," said the beadle. "No, I am only a Minimalist, I merely want the Minimum—that we save our own lives."

Israel Zangwill, *Ghetto Comedies*, 1907

Moral values, if they are to stand even a chance of broad observance across cultural boundaries, must be few in number and limited in scope. They must represent the simplest, most commonplace forms of mutual support, respect, and forbearance necessary for group survival. It must be possible to envisage them as present in communities as soon as human beings join in gathering and preparing food, in hunting and farming, in seeking shelter and raising families. Hampshire maintains that, while individuals and societies may always differ about what makes for the best kind of life, they also share certain needs that constitute "the minimum common basis for a tolerable human life."[18] Such a minimum must include a recognition of procedural justice—justice seen not as an abstract ideal but as shaping the basic forms of argument and negotiation on which communities rely in making choices. Whether in the council scenes in Homer's *Iliad*, where leaders met to settle conflicts and to decide between war and peace, or in debates in contemporary parliamentary bodies and international organizations, certain rudiments of procedure are necessary for decision making: recognizing differing points of view, hearing and weighing arguments, and striving for a modicum of impartiality. While these rudiments hardly guarantee the fairness or the wisdom of the outcome, they provide "the core of a thin notion of minimum procedural justice."[19]

18. *Innocence and Experience*, 32–33.
19. Ibid., 14.

But why should the claim that certain values have arisen in most societies serve, by itself, to single out those values as legitimate or admirable ones? After all, slavery has also been practiced in many parts of the world, as has the maltreatment of women; yet the frequency of these practices guarantees them no such status. Or, as Voltaire puts the question, after asserting that no one has ever doubted that justice demands that one ought to give back what one has borrowed and promised to return: "One could object to me that the consent of people in all periods and all countries is no proof of truth. All peoples have believed in magic, in spells, in demons, in apparitions, in the influence of stars, and in hundreds of similar inanities. Might it not be the same with respect to what is just and unjust?"[20]

That analogy doesn't work, Voltaire writes, because, in the first place, not all have believed in such chimeras, least of all the majority of wise people; and, in the second place, such beliefs are far from being necessary for human survival, unlike the acceptance of rules of justice. Similarly, neither slavery nor the maltreatment of women has been universally accepted, much less thought everywhere necessary to survival. It is clearly the case that many societies have not only fostered profoundly unjust practices but also held a number of them in common during much of their history. From a minimalist perspective, however, the point is not to deny that such societies can survive, nor to affirm that most communities fully honor even rudimentary demands of justice, but to make the narrower claim that not even the smallest groups could survive without *any* requirements of justice such as those Hampshire specifies.

In addition to at least rudimentary rules, Hampshire holds that a set of fundamental duties and obligations is worked out in every society, though taking different forms in each: "the obligations of love and friendship, of duties of benevolence, or at least of

---

20. *Le Philosophe ignorant* (1767), in *Voltaire: Mélanges* (Paris: Bibliothèque de la Pléiade, 1965), 913. My translation. Voltaire adds, in speaking of the universal acceptance of views regarding borrowing, that of course there may be exceptions, when one has reason to believe that harm might result from doing so, "as when the person to whom I owe two million will use it to enslave his country."

restraints against harm and destruction of life."[21] This list, stressing both benevolence and nonmaleficence, may nevertheless still be too "maximalist" for the purposes of a minimalist ethics, in referring to *obligations* of love and friendship. The obligations that the ideals of love and friendship engender are difficult to specify even within societies and can hardly be prescribed cross-culturally, unlike the restraint against the destruction of life. Few who heard of the campaigns by mothers for the return of their "disappeared" in Argentina and other nations had the slightest difficulty understanding their plight. But whereas we can invoke a right not to be subjected to such treatment, whether by fellow citizens or by strangers, we can claim no comparable right to be treated with friendship or love.

Even as Hampshire's list of duties and obligations may be too maximalist, it is in another respect too minimalist. It leaves out a pair of fundamental constraints long held indispensable for the survival of any collectivity, large or small: on deceit and on breaches of promise. All societies, no matter what their governance, have had to develop laws concerning deceit and breaches of faith. Without a modicum of trust, cooperation is undermined from the outset; those who erode trust by lying, cheating, or violating a promise, a contract, or a treaty inhibit the deliberative process to which Hampshire points as the most basic element of justice. Government leaders known to have few compunctions about breaking their word, for instance, will be distrusted no matter how scrupulously they claim to prohibit torture or assassination.

Michael Walzer has pursued the distinction between minimalist and maximalist moralities—characterizing the former type as thin, universal, and abstract, in contrast to the latter, which he sees as thick, rooted in the particular, and full-blooded. Using thin, universal concepts such as "truth" and "justice," he argues, we can respond to the cries for help from persons in very different cultures whose basic rights have been violated; and, by comparing such responses and the abuses occasioning them, we may be able to

---

21. *Innocence and Experience*, 32–33. See also Robert M. Adams, "Religious Ethics in a Pluralistic Society," in Gene Outka and John P. Reeder, Jr., eds., *Prospects for a Common Morality* (Princeton: Princeton University Press, 1993), 53–72.

understand what they have in common: "Perhaps the end product of this effort will be a set of standards to which all societies can be held—negative injunctions, most likely, rules against murder, deceit, torture, oppression, and tyranny."[22]

Walzer argues that minimalist meanings are embedded in maximalist moralities, different for each culture. Oppression and injustice can be criticized from a minimalist perspective; but even when we adopt such a perspective, we move quickly beyond such minimum standards: "The hope that minimalism, grounded and expanded, might serve the cause of a universal critique is a false hope. Minimalism makes for a certain limited, though important and heartening, solidarity. It doesn't make for a full-blooded universal doctrine."[23] Minimalism, for Walzer, cannot offer the basis for a common program; it is more likely to be hastily brought to bear against a common enemy. If so, however, minimalism cannot come anywhere near sufficing for the level of international cooperation made necessary by the threats societies now face. Would some form of maximalism serve this purpose better? Neither Walzer nor others taking up this issue have maintained that one or more versions of maximalism are more likely to do so than has been the case up to now.

The theologian Hans Küng argues, in *Projekt Weltethos*, for "a minimum fundamental ethical consensus" in response to the present crises.[24] Without such a consensus, "a common existence worthy of human beings is possible neither in a smaller nor in a larger community." According to Küng, certain precepts are held in common by all major world religions: (1) not to kill; (2) not to lie; (3) not to steal; (4) not to engage in fornication; (5) to honor one's parents and love one's children. These precepts can be used, he suggests, as standards by which to judge not only political tyranny, corruption, and infringements of human rights, but also religious practices such as those of human sacrifice, temple prostitution, and inquisitions.

While the treatments of minimalist values by Hart, Hampshire, Walzer, and Küng overlap, they offer no unanimity regarding either

22. Walzer, "Moral Minimalism," 9.
23. Ibid., 10.
24. *Projekt Weltethos*, chap. 2.

the extent or the practical uses of such values. The same is true of the texts setting forth common values discussed in Chapter 1, as well as of the central principles of conduct stressed in systems of normative ethics and in the texts of the major world religions to which Küng refers. Yet if we step back to adopt, in turn, a minimalist perspective on these different treatments, we find that the area of overlap can provide a basis from which to pursue further debate. At the very least, the great majority of views stress, first, duties of mutual support and loyalty and, second, a limited set of constraints on specific forms of violence and dishonesty; third, however different the methods worked out to deal with conflicts regarding these values, most views reflect the "thin notion of procedural justice" of which Hampshire writes.

Thus pared down, these forms of support, constraints, and procedural prescriptions can provide the rudiments of a shared minimalist ethics. True, they are rooted in particular communities and often seen, by members, as limited in application to their fellow members. But together, these values provide a basis and the possibility of a common language for critical inquiry and dialogue across cultural boundaries about how they might be extended, and about more comprehensive maximalist requirements and ideals. Unlike Benda's more general and abstract appeals to truth, justice, reason, and humanity, these minimalist values can provide particular criteria for evaluating practices at the individual as at the collective level, in private life as in public and professional life, at home and abroad.

What of the retort that a minimalist set of moral constraints still fails to provide such criteria because, however ubiquitous, the constraints are differently interpreted, depending on personal and cultural norms? The biblical injunction not to bear false witness about one's neighbor can be interpreted from the narrowest point of view as concerning only testimony in court and only about one's actual neighbors, all the way to the broadest prohibition of all deceit. The debates about hunting, abortion, and capital punishment revolve around what constitutes murder. And most forms of criticism by a family member, colleague, or friend can be interpreted as constituting betrayal by those at whom the criticism is aimed. A minimalist perspective need not, however, exclude these distinctions. It does not require the unanimity of interpretation that will surely always be out of reach, so much as an exploration of those evaluations that already command the widest possible agreement.

Minimalism calls, therefore, for us to begin by asking: out of all the possible forms and degrees of violence, deceit, and breaches of faith, which ones can be agreed upon most easily from the outset as in need of constraint? We may never agree about the boundaries of deceit, much less about all the possible meanings of "truth," yet we know quite well when we are telling an outright lie. And whatever the kinds of action that we may see as constituting unjust deprivation of life—leading us to differ on subjects such as hunting, abortion, or capital punishment—far fewer would disagree about clear-cut cases of police shooting into an unarmed crowd. The same is true of unambiguous violations of arms accords or well-documented forms of embezzlement.

Another objection to a minimalist approach concerns its piece-meal, incomplete nature, both in theory and in practice. Why not start out with one's own maximalist views, say about religion or politics, and suggest or impose them as the blueprint for a shared ethics, rather than seeking out a minimalist basis for discussions with holders of a great many perspectives? Or even begin with the most cosmic injunctions, such as that by Václav Havel, urging that "We must discover a new respect for what transcends us: for the universe, for the earth, for nature, for life, and for reality. Our respect for other people, for other nations, and for other cultures can only grow from a humble respect for the cosmic order and from an awareness that we are a part of it, that we share in it and that nothing of what we do is lost, but rather becomes part of the eternal memory of being, where it is judged."[25] Surely both directions will be helpful in debating the moral issues we face—beginning from the most abstract and general principles or the most down-to-earth ones. The danger arises when only one perspective is taken to be the correct one.

25. Václav Havel, Commencement Address, Harvard University, June 8, 1995, reprinted in *Harvard Gazette*, June 15, 1995, pp. 9–10.

The greater the certainty attached to any one maximalist doctrine, the stronger the reluctance to allow any debate or challenge. Such convictions, when linked with longing for some all-embracing system or for some total transformation of society, have traditionally represented the greatest obstacles to a stepwise, limited, and admittedly imperfect minimalist approach to social change. The very terms *minimalist* and *maximalist* originated as translations of the Russian terms *Menshevik* and *Bolshevik*, contrasting reformist and revolutionary approaches to change.[26] But revolutionary maximalism is no more capable than other maximalist visions of achieving widespread cross-cultural acceptance. To insist on total transformation merely blocks the possibility of incremental progress which, if incomplete, is still valuable. Our century bears witness to the ease with which advocates of total transformation violate even the most fundamental moral values in the service of their particular goals.

Beyond Minimalism

> *No tribe could hold together if murders, robbery, treachery, &c.,*
> *were common; consequently such crimes within the limits of the*
> *same tribe "are branded with everlasting infamy"; but excite no*
> *such sentiment beyond these limits. . . .*
> *As man advances in civilization, and small tribes are united*
> *into larger communities, the simplest reason would tell each indi-*
> *vidual that he ought to extend his social instincts and sympathies*
> *to all the members of the same nation, though personally unknown*
> *to him. This point being once reached, there is only an artificial*
> *barrier to prevent his sympathies extending to the men of all*
> *nations and races.*
>
> Charles Darwin, *The Descent of Man*

Artificial or no, Darwin had to admit that the barrier to extending an individual's sympathies universally was a potent one in practice:

26. *Oxford English Dictionary; Webster's Third New International Dictionary.*

"If, indeed, such men are separated from him by great differences in appearance or habits, experience unfortunately shows us how long it is before we look at them as our fellow-creatures."[27] It is this familiar experience that generates the most serious practical objection to searching for a shared minimalist ethics. What earthly reason might there be to believe that such an ethics could make a difference in practice? After all, constraints on killing and fraud are hard enough to maintain within communities, as are basic forms of procedural justice and mutual support. Why should people, even if they recognized values similar to their own in other cultures, agree to observe them, either within or outside the frontiers of their own states?

When viewed from a minimalist perspective, such an objection must once again elicit both partial agreement and demurral. Of course it is unlikely that people will change thus automatically, and of course many may not change at all. I shall return to this objection in Chapters 4 and 5; but I want to suggest, here, that it should not be taken to invalidate the search for a shared ethics in its own right. It matters, for purposes of responding more forcefully to collective threats to well-being and survival, whether or not increasing numbers of individuals come to perceive basic values as held in common in more societies than their own. So long as the search for shared values continues, and so long as the most fundamental ones already command a sufficiently widespread allegiance to make possible more concerted collective action, there remains a basis from which to continue.

The growth of international human rights advocacy in the years since World War II offers a striking demonstration of the cumulative power of such leverage. In *The Code of Peace*, Dorothy Jones reports on the evolution of international standards of conduct and analyzes the myriad incremental shifts leading from initial rhetoric to partial implementation. When human rights were first mentioned, at Versailles in 1919, and for decades thereafter, they were routinely excluded from international treaties. Most government

27. Charles Darwin, *The Descent of Man* (1859; Princeton: Princeton University Press, 1981), 101.

leaders regarded the status of human rights within their frontiers as a uniquely internal matter, and their self-serving orating on the subject was regarded by observers (including Benda) as strictly rhetorical. Seven decades later, however, Jones points out, the rhetoric of human rights

> had proved to be a stimulus for action, and that action could not be ignored. . . . What was clear was that people, especially in the Eastern bloc states, had seized on the rules that the states said should apply and demanded that the states apply them. The states of the West had joined the campaign, using state-level tools of diplomatic pressure and then, at the review conferences, public disclosures of human rights violations—a move that threw the initiative back to the people again.[28]

In this respect, therefore, shoulder-shrugging at what seemed mere rhetoric about justice and rights may once have reflected healthy skepticism but is no longer sufficient. Nor is a strictly relativistic view of the degree of possible understanding between societies an adequate basis for action. As the media disseminate images worldwide of atrocities from places such as Tienanmen Square, Kurdistan, Burma, Croatia, or Somalia, it becomes ever more difficult to maintain that the victims are somehow so culturally different from the viewing public that their plight cannot be evaluated from the outside, or so completely in the power of the state in which they happen to have been born that outsiders are duty-bound to look the other way.

To be sure, many governments still violate their people's rights not to be tortured, enslaved, or arbitrarily deprived of life—rights that form the cornerstone of the 1948 Universal Declaration of Human Rights. But it is noteworthy that not one such government dares offer legal justification for doing so. As Henry J. Steiner has pointed out, even if government leaders "claim moral justification for such conduct because of temporary exigent circumstances, they do not dispute what a full realization of the right [not to be arbitrarily deprived of life or subjected to torture] would entail."[29]

---

28. *Code of Peace*, 161–62.
29. "Political Participation as a Human Right," *Harvard Human Rights Yearbook* 1 (spring 1988): 82.

Even critics willing to consider the urgency of seeking a shared minimalist ethics might object, however, that it cannot suffice as a basis from which to address more intractable collective problems, which elicit far less agreement, even in principle, than violations of the most fundamental human rights. Political and religious authorities who deny the right to freedom of conscience, for instance, may regard advocacy of such a right as immoral or counterproductive. And as for the entitlements listed in the Universal Declaration of Human Rights—to adequate nourishment, schooling, and shelter, for example—they are flagrantly denied even in many wealthy societies. The debate over distributive justice will be exacerbated in the decades to come as more and more hundreds of millions of human beings come to suffer deprivations that make a mockery of the rhetoric about such entitlements.

These critics have a strong case. It is far from clear that we shall see the same progression from rhetoric to acknowledgment and increasing implementation with respect to such entitlements as has taken place, over recent decades, in the case of fundamental political freedoms. Widespread adherence to minimalist moral constraints such as those on violence and fraud won't suffice for generating the required changes. Even if government leaders and all others were exemplary in honoring these constraints, this would not by itself suffice to combat famines such as those now spreading in many regions in Africa. Nor would adherence to the procedural and cooperative practices that also form a necessary part of a shared minimalist ethics suffice to generate the necessary momentum on their own.

As for the basic ideals of support and loyalty that represent the first element of a shared minimalist ethics, they call precisely on those "social instincts and sympathies" which, as Darwin pointed out, are so especially difficult to extend beyond narrow group boundaries. This is the more true whenever extending them demands sacrifices on the home front; and even more when, as in a number of Asian and African nations, exceptionally high birth rates add inexorably to the number of individuals needing to be included within the range of such broadened sympathies.

The same difficulties, from the point of view of the adequacy of a minimalist ethics, arise with respect to the interlocking environmental problems threatening the future and exacerbating present poverty and suffering: pollution, desertification, destruction of rain forests, extinction of species, disposal of toxic chemicals, and—again—population growth. While international cooperation in cutting back sulfur dioxide emissions and regional environmental cleanup has brought about notable progress, the inadequacy of present responses in most other areas is daunting.[30] To move forward fast enough with respect to those areas, enlarging the reach of basic moral constraints and procedural justice will not suffice; and extended sympathies are hardest of all to achieve.

The most striking progress in international collaboration on environmental issues (though, once again, still far from meeting present needs) has taken place with respect to ozone depletion—a threat much more clearly perceived as affecting each nation's immediate self-interest. While it took seven decades for nations to shift from rhetoric to concerted international action on human rights, it took fewer than seven years to mobilize such action with respect to the damage being done to Earth's ozone layer. Beginning in 1987, governments have repeatedly agreed to step up the speed with which they act to cut back on the consumption of chlorofluorocarbons and other causes of ozone depletion.

To the extent that peoples and governments recognize that they cannot meet such a potent threat alone and that not only their descendants but they themselves are at ever-growing risk, negotiations move more rapidly and mutual aid comes to be perceived as imperative. Long-range concern for the self-interest of others is much harder to mobilize. It requires extrapolating from the most imminent risks affecting one's society to those posed by global levels of poverty, population growth, and environmental deterioration, and considering how much the failure to deal more far-sightedly with

---

30. See Hilary French, "After the Earth Summit: The Future of Environmental Governance," Worldwatch Paper 107, March 1992, Table 1, "International Environmental Governance: Some Notable Accomplishments and Remaining Challenges."

the latter already affects the self-interest of even the most prosperous communities and nations. As Chernobyl and the AIDS epidemic have once again demonstrated, societies cannot wall themselves off: "lifeboat ethics" makes less sense than ever.

How might the search for a common ethics contribute to a more forceful collective response to such problems? It will be important to examine the diplomatic, cultural, and other ways in which the "social instincts and sympathies" of which Darwin spoke can be extended in practice, since this element of a minimalist ethics is by far the hardest to develop across cultural boundaries. To the extent, moreover, that a minimalist ethics leads us to take seriously the need to engage others in a discussion about our common fate, we shall be treating them as real partners rather than as distant peoples of little concern to us. We might then discern our common humanity *in practice:* not by reflecting on whether some property is or is not "essentially human," but by considering how we have to think of others if we are to acknowledge their right to participate in our reflections about the threats we all confront, and our corresponding responsibility to respond to these threats in ways we can justify to them.

In a comment on the original article on which the present chapter is based, Amartya Sen asks whether the problems of cross-cultural cooperation, difficult for the reasons I discuss, are substantially altered by the existence of considerable *internal* diversity within practically every society:

> There are modernists in traditional societies, skeptics in fundamentalist cultures, liberals and radicals in conservative communities. The pressure for change need not come only from outside. While official suppression of heterodoxy in some countries does reveal international differences in political tolerance, they also point to the existence of substantial diversities *within* the respective nations, since repression of opposition would be otherwise redundant. While diversity and opposition may foster strife within nations, would Sissela Bok agree that they may in the long run provide more hope for the development of shared international ethics?[31]

31. "Three Questions," 26.

As internal conflict and hatred devastate increasing numbers of societies in the post–Cold War era, it is especially urgent to pose such questions about the conditions under which domestic diversity helps or hurts the prospects for cross-cultural dialogue. Other things being equal, societies that protect dissent and encourage nonviolent efforts toward accommodation are better equipped to take part in similar processes on the international level. And when debates become so embittered and venomous on the home front as to threaten a society's domestic peace and the rule of law, its voice is correspondingly weakened in international discussions.

The struggle within societies thus beleaguered is not only between particular religious or political traditions as to which one will win out. It is also a struggle within each of the different traditions about how, if at all, to live with, and accommodate to, disagreement, whether from within or without. A minimalist ethics can play a crucial role in efforts to explore the possibility for such accommodation. It can offer a starting point for dialogue and debate as well as criteria for when conduct, whether on the part of adversaries or of colleagues, violates the most basic moral values stressed in all traditions, though too rarely thought to apply to dissidents and outsiders. Intellectuals on all sides of such debates can play a crucial role by articulating humane conceptions of what adversaries have in common, of how to confront differences on such a basis, and of how to honor both uniqueness and diversity within the bounds of basic moral values.

Sen also asks, in his commentary, whether a stress on behavior ought not to have priority over an inquiry concerning values, even though he was very much in sympathy with the kind of critical search for common values that had been presented. Can it be argued, he asks,

> that the urgent need now is not so much for any universal set of *values*, but for general acceptance of some modes of *behaviour* (even if that shared acceptance is grounded on thoroughly divergent values)? Isn't there larger hope of such behavioural concordance than of the more-than-minimalist valuational congruence for which Bok argues, especially since socially achievable results such as survival, peace, prosperity, or general freedom help the pursuit of many altogether

distinct values? Would it be, then, right to put more emphasis on seeking behavioural correspondence for instrumental reasons rather than on the search for substantive unanimity of values?[32]

Sen is right to point out that what is most urgently needed is acceptance of certain modes of behavior—namely those most conducive to furthering collective survival. By itself, widespread agreement on values, such as the constraint on violence, matters little so long as the values are not observed in practice. Indeed, some of the bloodiest persecutions of our day, within societies as across borders, are accompanied by daily protestations of nonviolence and the desire for peace.

Even where such values are observed in practice, views differ thoroughly, as Sen points out, about how they are to be justified or derived. Many justify them by appealing to the instrumental reasons Sen proposes; others may see them as ordained by supernatural authority, as consistent with natural law, or as rooted in a biological imperative. While I share Sen's concern with reaching agreement on modes of behavior, I am therefore reluctant to limit in advance the kinds of reasons for endorsing them to instrumental ones. To serve as a basis for agreement about behavior among members of different cultures, a minimalist ethics should be open to all who are willing to subscribe to it, whatever their reasons or justifications might be for doing so.

A long-standing objection to such a view, however, holds that once one agrees that justifications for values differ, one must also recognize that no set of values or forms of commonly accepted behavior could possibly serve as a basis for the kind of cross-cultural and intra-cultural debate I have advocated: for how can there be such a common basis without commonly accepted foundations for moral beliefs? It is to this objection that I turn in Chapter 3.

32. Ibid.

What Basis for Morality?

A Minimalist Approach

Principles are not less sacred because their duration cannot be guaranteed. Indeed, the very desire for guarantees that our values are eternal and secure in some objective heaven is perhaps only a craving for the certainties of childhood or the absolute values of our primitive past. "To realize the relative validity of one's convictions," said an admirable writer of our time, "and yet stand for them unflinchingly, is what distinguishes a civilized man from a barbarian."

Isaiah Berlin, "Two Concepts of Liberty," 1958

Acceptance of common values (at any rate some irreducible minimum of them) enters our conception of a normal human being. This serves to distinguish such notions as the foundations of human morality . . . from such other notions as custom, or tradition, or law, or manners, or fashion, or etiquette.

Isaiah Berlin, Four Essays on Liberty, 1969

How fully can the views expressed in the two passages above be reconciled? Many insist that one has to opt either for rejecting all lasting guarantees for moral principles or for accepting common values as a foundation of morality, but that one cannot make both claims in a consistent manner. Berlin would disagree—rightly as I hope to show in this chapter. I shall set forth different claims about the foundations for morality that give rise to such disagreement and explore, in so doing, alternative responses to the uncontestable tension exhibited by Berlin's two passages between, on the one hand, thorough skepticism regarding the existence of permanent, objective, and universal moral values and, on the other, a conviction that at least some actions and practices must still be judged as just or unjust, humane or inhumane, right or wrong, wherever they occur.

Foundations, Rhetoric, and Metaphors

The statement that Berlin attributes to the "admirable writer" has initial appeal for anyone troubled by the tension regarding foundations. On closer scrutiny, however, the value-laden terms "admirable," "convictions," "unflinchingly," "civilized," and "barbarian" merely help to disguise rather than to overcome that tension.[1] The posture of standing by one's convictions "unflinchingly," for example, hints at moral heroism; but exactly why *should* such an unflinching stance be a mark of civilization? Surely, both the nature of the convictions and what is done to uphold them must matter. Otherwise, might not a Caligula or a Goebbels qualify as civilized rather than barbarian? And why should anyone be so presumptuous as to label as "barbarian" the vast majority of human beings who either believe their convictions to be fully valid or whose stance, regardless of whether or not they do, is less than unflinching?

Attributing moral worth as inherent in an unflinching stance for one's personal convictions proves nothing by itself. And the rhetoric about who counts as "a civilized man" or "a barbarian" is equally unpersuasive in the absence of moral justification. But the call for justification brings back into question the felt contradiction or tension that the oft-cited words of the "admirable writer" merely paper over. How else, then, might one address that tension? How

---

1. The "admirable writer" quoted by Berlin was Joseph Schumpeter. For comments on this passage, see Richard Rorty, *Contingency, Irony, and Solidarity* (New York: Cambridge University Press, 1989), 45–52, and Michael Sandel, ed., *Liberalism and Its Critics* (New York: New York University Press, 1984), 8.

might one either justify both Berlin's pluralism and his affirmation of some foundation for human morality, or else accept the former while convincingly disproving the latter?

The very possibility of such a foundation or justification, long debated throughout the history of philosophy, has been increasingly challenged in recent decades, often in the name of "antifoundationalism." Coined in the 1970s, this neologism is by now familiar in literary, epistemological, metaphysical, and moral debates (though it is not yet, to the best of my knowledge, to be found in any general or philosophical dictionary).[2]

Antifoundationalists, taking up the perennial philosophical debates concerning the possibility of secure foundations for knowledge and morality, have rejected as "foundationalist" a great number of religious and secular moral doctrines that affirm such foundations. The point of departure for antifoundationalists has generally been to deny that there can be absolutely secure insights grounding our knowledge, such as Descartes' *cogito, ergo sum*; a more general antifoundationalist critique addresses all claims that our moral or other views have any basis whatsoever beyond purely subjective and contingent experience.

The latter critique, which can issue in a form of ethical nihilism, is too rarely set apart from the former one, which addresses Cartesian-type claims to absolute certainty, and equally rarely employed in such a way as to distinguish between foundational claims in the realms of epistemology, metaphysics, and ethics. As a result,

---

2. For recent discussions of foundationalism in epistemology, see the entries by Robert Audi, Laurence Bonjour, and Richard Fumerton, as well as the introduction by Louis P. Pojman to "Theories of Justification (I) Foundationalism and Coherentism," in Louis B. Pojman, *The Theory of Knowledge: Classical and Contemporary Readings* (Belmont, Calif.: Wadsworth Publishing Co., 1993), pt. 5. For discussions of foundationalism and justification in ethics, see the articles in *The Monist* 76:3 (1993) on the "General Topic" of "Justification in Ethics." For more general discussions of foundations and foundationalism, see Iris Murdoch, *Metaphysics as a Guide to Morals* (New York: Allen Lane, Penguin Press, 1992), 185–216; John P. Reeder, Jr., "Foundations without Foundationalism," in Gene Outka and John P. Reeder, Jr., eds., *Prospects for a Common Morality* (Princeton: Princeton University Press, 1993), 191–214; Tom Rockmore and Beth J. Singer, eds., *Antifoundationalism Old and New* (Philadelphia: Temple University Press, 1992); R. Rorty, *Essays on Heidegger and Others* (Cambridge: Cambridge University Press, 1991), 10–11; Reiner Schürmann, *Heidegger on Being and Acting: From Principles to Anarchy* (Bloomington: Indiana University Press, 1990), 1–7, 35.

antifoundationalists have taken aim at doctrines as different as Platonism, Cartesianism, theories of practical reason, religious fundamentalism, and Natural Law—whether the latter is seen as having been, in the words of Cicero, "engraved in our hearts" or rather, following Thomas Aquinas, held to have been promulgated by the Christian God.[3] It is perhaps no wonder that attacks aiming at so many, and such different, targets have tended to be carried out in a scattershot manner, lumping together numerous claims rarely if ever advocated together by any one thinker or in any one doctrine and then proceeded to condemn several of these claims together through a process of "guilt by association." Among the claims lumped together are groupings of the following:

1. that certain moral values are divinely ordained
2. that they are part of the natural order
3. that they are eternally valid
4. that they are valid without exception
5. that they can be directly known by any rational being
6. that they can be perceived by a "moral sense"
7. that they exist independently of human beings
8. that they are objective rather than subjective
9. that they are held in common by all human beings
10. that they have had to be worked out in all human societies

These claims are hardly identical. No tight link binds them, forcing holders of any one of them to accept all the others. Most have been debated, and their intricate relations examined, since the beginnings of theology and moral philosophy: they clearly call for independent scrutiny in the debate over foundationalism as well. In the absence of such scrutiny, attacks on any view asserting some foundation for morality often simply conflate the different claims by rejecting or placing in doubt at least one of them and then concluding without further ado that there can be no such foundation whatsoever.

---

3. Cicero, *De Re Publica, III* (57 B.C.), xxii, 33; Thomas Aquinas, *Summa Theologica* (1272), II, I, questions 90–94.

Most commonly, critics of foundations take a leap, Nietzschean-style, from asserting that there is no God and that there cannot therefore exist divinely ordained moral laws or values (rejecting claim 1) to concluding that there can be no secure foundations whatsoever for morality. Alternatively, the first four claims are rejected, and, since these are often held to ground claims 5–8, the latter are then in turn set aside more summarily. Still other attacks deny claims 3, 4, and 8—holding that certain moral values are eternally valid, valid without exception, and objective rather than subjective—and proceed to dismiss all foundations for morality as nonexistent.[4] The same procedure of summary dismissal often begins by rejecting as unprovable claim 7—that certain values exist independently of human beings—or by discarding as empirically false or unprovable claim 2, that certain moral values are part of the natural order.

Why should claims about the foundation of knowledge or of morality appear such easy targets for summary dismissal? A central reason is that the metaphor of "foundations" is such a powerful one in its own right. The more it is invoked to suggest solid support, the more routinely it also invites questions of infinite regress, just as rejections of the existence of rock-solid foundations invite images of unmooring and of drifting. During the Enlightenment, debates about the effects for morality and religion of either asserting or denying such firm foundations came to a crux. Repeatedly, the same imagery, taken from John Locke, was invoked on both sides of the debate.

Elephants on Tortoises

If anyone should be asked what is the subject wherein colour or weight inheres, he would have nothing to say, but the solid

---

4. See, for an example of such argumentation, Barbara Herrnstein Smith, *Contingencies of Value: Alternative Perspectives for Critical Theory* (Cambridge: Harvard University Press, 1988), 150 *et seq.* For a cogent review of these and related claims, see Judith Wagner DeCew, "Moral Conflicts and Ethical Relativism," *Ethics* 101 (October 1990): 27–41.

> *extended parts; and if he were demanded what it is that solidity*
> *and extension adhere in, he would not be in a much better case*
> *than the Indian . . . who, saying that the world was supported*
> *by a great elephant, was asked what the elephant rested on; to*
> *which his answer was: a great tortoise; but being again pressed*
> *to know what gave support to the broad-backed tortoise, replied:*
> *something, he knew not what.*
>
> John Locke, *An Essay Concerning Human Understanding*

Locke uses the metaphor of an elephant resting on tortoises to illustrate the difficulties besetting efforts to convey the meaning of "substance." Much like inquiries into the foundations of knowledge or of morality, such efforts almost inevitably bring to mind questions of infinite regress. In discussing the temptation to imagine that many simple ideas conveyed by the senses must inhere in some one substratum that we call "substance," Locke indicates that we talk, in such cases, like children, giving names to the supposed but unknown supports of those qualities we find existing which we imagine cannot subsist without something to support them; he adds that the "true import of the word [*substantia*] is, in plain English, standing under or upholding."[5]

It is natural, when making analogies to physical foundations—in epistemology and ethics as in metaphysics—to ask what, in turn, holds them up. Repeated questions of this kind easily issue in debates about whether there are tortoises "all the way down." Thus Denis Diderot cited Locke's passage to convey the uselessness of any hypothesis attempting to explain all that is incomprehensible in nature by reference to the concept of a deity no less incomprehensible. "First confess your ignorance, and spare me the elephant and the tortoise."[6] In turn, Jean-Jacques Rousseau used Diderot's imagery to reinforce the argument made by Julie, in *Julie or the New Heloise*, for the absolute need for religious belief as a foundation on

---

5. *An Essay Concerning Human Understanding* (1689), book 2, chap. XXIII, sec. 2.
6. *Lettres sur les aveugles*, in *Oeuvres philosophiques* (1749; Paris: Garnier, 1956), 120. My translation.

which to practice virtue: "It is not enough, believe me, that virtue should be the basis of your conduct, if you do not establish this basis itself on an unshakable foundation. Remember those Indians who view the world as carried by a great elephant, and that elephant by a tortoise; and when one asks them on what the tortoise stands, they no longer know what to say."[7]

Even as Rousseau accused the "philosophes" who refused to base morality on religion of having no foundation in God's edicts and no barriers, as a consequence, against crime of every kind, so Diderot argued that those who sought a foundation in anything as incomprehensible as God's desires were themselves open to endorsing every crime in the name of religion. The story of the elephant and the tortoises could be used to support such contradictory conclusions in part because of the very immediacy and force with which it delineates metaphors of supporting, being founded upon, and upholding, and with which it raises, in turn, questions about infinite regress.

When the story is shorn of the explication that Locke accorded it, as in the accounts by Diderot and Rousseau, these connotations are especially likely to short-circuit argumentation regarding the foundations of morality. Instead, they facilitate conclusions that take the form of an ultimatum: Show me foundations all the way down, or admit that there are none!

Once you press the analogy thus hastily between physical foundations and the foundations claimed for morality or any other theoretical construct, a more general spatial supposition often slips in: that "underneath" everything that is not to be regarded as merely arbitrary, there must be something else. The inference then lies near at hand that either the need for some impossible absolutist "rock bottom" or else infinite regress threatens *any* foundational claim.

This inference is the more tempting as many religious foundational doctrines do indeed assert such absolute guarantees for the

---

7. *Julie ou La Nouvelle Heloise* (1761), part III, letter XX. My translation. For a discussion of the issue of foundations for morality in French philosophy during the Enlightenment, see Jacques Domenech, *L'Ethique des lumières: Les fondements de la morale dans la philosophie française du XVIIIè siècle* (Paris: Librairie J. Vrin, 1989). For recent discussions, see the essays collected in Jean-Pierre Changeux, ed., *Fondements naturels de l'éthique* (Paris: Edition Odile Jacob, 1993).

foundations of morality, in the form of claim 1, above, invoking divine edict to render them immune to the threat of infinite regress. But it is a mistake for antifoundationalists simply to deploy against more limited views of possible foundations for morality the same arguments that they take to invalidate religious and other doctrines that postulate absolute, eternal, and measureless warranty for morality. For no matter how strong and how lasting the support of the more limited foundations may be for the purposes they are meant to serve, they will never, any more than physical foundations, satisfy such absolutist criteria.

Another, and to my mind more plausible, way to ask about the possibility of a shared basis of moral values for practical purposes in addressing common problems is to adopt the minimalist approach discussed in Chapters 1 and 2: one that seeks out the values that are in fact broadly shared, without requiring either absolute guarantees for them or unanimity regarding them. Such a minimalist inquiry can take as its starting point claims 9 and 10 above—concerning values held in common by all human beings that have had to be worked out in all human societies—while simply bracketing particular views regarding claims 1–8, for purposes of finding common ground.

There is no need, for such purposes, to abandon references to the concept of "foundation(s)." But it will help to view that concept, with all its metaphorical baggage, in a larger context that includes the concepts of "ground" or "grounds." The latter concepts present fewer temptations to seek "tortoises all the way down"; indeed, many of the metaphors relating to "ground(s)" have to do with human stances and actions on Earth's surface, not with probing its depths; with dialogue, debate, and conflict rather than with absolute certainty; and with the search for accommodation and consensus rather than with unanimity. Dictionaries link "ground" in the singular with the solid surface of Earth or its soil and with actions such as "seeking common ground," "gaining ground," "standing one's ground," and "shifting one's ground." In the plural, "grounds" can refer to reasons offered for an argument, belief, or action, as in the expressions "grounds for divorce" or "grounds for suspicion." Likewise, "to ground" means not just to place or set on the ground, but also to substantiate, to justify, to supply with basic and essential information.

The conceptual family of "ground(s)" may therefore be more compatible than that of "foundation(s)" with a minimalist effort to seek a *basis*, or common ground, for broad-gauged communication and cooperation across cultural boundaries. Such an approach brackets all requirements for foundations that go "all the way down" or for singling out some one religious or metaphysical doctrine affirming one or more of the ten claims. It seeks to identify, instead, a minimal set of values offering grounds in other senses of the word: not only as providing reasons for a judgment, an action, a choice, a manner of proceeding, or a way of life, but also as creating a socially fashioned basis indispensable for communication and deliberation about such matters in all moral traditions.

Indeed, the concept of "basis" may serve such a minimalist aim still better than either "foundation(s)" or "ground(s)," while overlapping with them in relevant respects. Among the senses listed for "basis" in dictionaries, several seem especially pertinent from a minimalist point of view: "the chief or most stable component of anything"; "the main constituent, fundamental ingredient of something"; "that on which anything is reared, constructed, or established, and by which its constitution or operation is determined; groundwork, footing"; "a set of principles laid down or agreed upon as the ground of negotiation, or action."[8]

Onora O'Neill has set forth a constructivist ethics without foundations, in *Constructions of Reason*. Such an ethics can be firm and carefully constructed without being in any sense arbitrary. We have a ready analogy, she suggests, in space architecture:

> Space satellites do not have "foundations" or identifiable "higher" or "lower" parts, but their parts must interlock: Their construction is not arbitrary. Constructivist accounts of ethical requirements also propose no single foundation, yet do not appeal to a mere plurality of moral intuitions without order. As with other constructions, the parts

8. From the Greek word *basis:* a stepping; a step, walk; that whereon which one steps, ground: a pedestal.

are to be put together with an eye to the coherence and functioning of the structure. The art is to use minimal and plausible assumptions about human rationality and agency to construct an account of ethical requirements that is rich and strong enough to guide action and reflection.[9]

A constructivist basis for morality thus interpreted calls for no extrahuman or superhuman guarantees of objectivity or absoluteness. To the extent that it is a minimalist basis, it offers, rather, a common groundwork or footing upon which to undertake dialogue, debate, and negotiations within and between otherwise disparate traditions: a set of values that can be agreed upon as a starting point for negotiation or action. However differently participants may view this set of values as itself founded or justified (say by reference to one or more of claims 1–8) it represents the "chief or most stable component" of what they can hold in common.

Pluralism and Shared Values from a Minimalist Perspective

Can such an approach to the basis or the foundation(s) or ground(s) for morality reconcile the views expressed in the two statements by Isaiah Berlin? Can it encompass both his broad-gauged pluralism and his insistence on shared values that allow for at least some cross-cultural judgments of right and wrong? In the first passage, setting aside as legacies from childhood the craving for absolute values and for "guarantees that our values are eternal and secure in some objective heaven," Berlin can be seen as rejecting all of the claims 1–4, 7, and 8. His second passage, which asserts none of those claims, affirms, rather, a variation of claim 9: that the acceptance of at least some irreducible minimum of common moral values "enters our conception of a normal human being"; and that it is this

9. *Constructions of Reason: Explorations of Kant's Practical Philosophy* (Cambridge: Cambridge University Press, 1989), 194. See also John Rawls, *A Theory of Justice* (Cambridge: Harvard University Press, 1971) and *Political Liberalism* (New York: Columbia University Press, 1993).

characteristic of human beings that helps us to distinguish notions such as that of the foundations of human morality from others such as those of custom or law.

Viewed from a minimalist perspective, Berlin's two statements need express neither contradiction nor unsurmountable tension. Rather, they delineate a position that fits well with a minimalist approach to morality that brackets many larger claims about its foundations. But two questions arise for any view, such as Berlin's, that singles out "our conception of a normal human being" as delimiting those who accept common moral values; for normality and humanity have themselves been interpreted in different, sometimes incompatible, ways.

Widely differing assertions, first of all, about what characterizes normal human beings have flourished wherever groups have taken their particular moral doctrines to be so self-evident, so much a part of what it means to be human, as to require no further support or explanation. Such assertions of self-evidence have often been formulated (though not by Berlin) in terms of claims 5 and 6—that certain moral values can be directly known by any rational being and perceived by a "moral sense" analogous to the sense of vision whereby we perceive what is before our eyes. It has then seemed easy to conclude that anyone who experiences no such self-evidence must be outside the bounds of (adult) human normality, either unable or unwilling to perceive what is so indubitable to those who proclaim it. Among the last who could still make such calm, unblinking assertions about self-evidence were G. E. Moore, W. D. Ross, H. A. Prichard, and other British intuitionists in the first part of this century.[10] Thus Ross argued that "when we have reached sufficient mental maturity and have given sufficient attention to the proposition," the rightness of an act fulfilling a promise or effecting a just distribution of goods is self-evident, "just as a mathematical axiom, or the validity of a form of inference, is evident. The moral

---

10. Moore, *Principia Ethica* (Cambridge: Cambridge University Press, 1903); Ross, *The Right and the Good* (Oxford: Clarendon Press, 1930) and *Foundations of Ethics* (Oxford: Clarendon Press, 1939); Prichard, *Moral Obligation* (Oxford: Oxford University Press, 1949).

order expressed in these propositions is just as much part of the fundamental nature of the universe (and, we may add, of any possible universe in which there were moral agents at all) as is the spatial or numerical structure expressed in the axioms of geometry or arithmetic."[11]

Few now assume that what they take to be thus right must be self-evident to all persons of mental maturity, much less to all who satisfy "our conception of a normal human being." Because the concept of "a normal human being," like that of "mental maturity," is so vague, moreover, it has proved notoriously open to abuse, and never more than when morality is at issue. Anyone seen as deviating from such norms may then not merely be treated as deficient but exploited or punished as barbarian, degenerate, perverted, bestial, or subhuman.[12]

Because the concepts of normality and humanity have been so often invoked to legitimate such forms of exploitation and abuse, the temptation is strong simply to give them up. Why not abandon concepts so easy to invoke for purposes profoundly inimical to human well-being? Just as in the cases of "foundation(s)" and "ground(s)," however, such a temptation is to be resisted. Once we started on the path of clearing away concepts lending themselves to misuses, we would, to be consistent, have to abandon a great many other concepts—truth, justice, equality, and liberty among them—with no end in sight save the impoverishment of our moral vocabulary.

Instead of jettisoning the concepts of normality and humanity, a minimalist approach retains them for purposes of moral debate while expressly guarding against the dangers of using them to punish and exploit. Such an approach has to phrase claim 9, to the effect that certain moral values are held in common by all human beings, in less universal terms, and bracket all assertions of the self-evidence of these values or decrees as to what is and is not normal or somehow inherent in human nature.

---

11. *The Right and the Good*, 29–30.
12. See S. Bok, "Who Shall Count as a Human Being?" in Michael Goodman, ed., *What Is a Person?* (Clifton, N.J.: Humana Press, 1988), 213–28.

But even if claim 9 is envisaged strictly from such a minimalist perspective, a second question remains. Can this claim, by itself, suffice to support our understanding of the common foundations for morality? On what grounds can anyone affirm it who brackets one or more of claims 1–8 and the reflected self-evidence often thought to derive from them? It is one thing to regard moral values as generally acknowledged if we believe them to have been decreed by divine edict *for* all of humanity or otherwise to exist independently of human beings but to be available to them all, and quite another to do so in the absence of such beliefs. The more humanly rather than superhumanly or extrahumanly we take values to be grounded, the more unlikely it may seem that they should nevertheless be held thus in common.

How, then, might we account for such a common basis without relying on any combination of claims 1–8? For such a purpose, I suggest that claim 10—that certain moral values have had to be worked out in all human societies—must be brought in to support claim 9. Berlin relies on both in his most recent book, *The Crooked Timber of Humanity*, in qualifying his account of the inevitability of clashes of values within and among cultures by stressing that "all men have a basic sense of good and evil" and that there are, "if not universal values, at any rate a minimum without which societies could scarcely survive."[13]

To the extent that claim 10 is persuasive, it begins to provide the human rather than superhuman or extrahuman grounding that claim 9 requires before it can be convincingly asserted independently. Together, therefore, claims 9 and 10 will serve the purposes of a minimalist approach to the foundations of ethics better than claim 9 might on its own. The two can then provide the necessary basis, the common ground, for moral debate among holders of widely differing views regarding each of the remaining claims 1–8 and the basis, in turn, for more fruitful and rigorous cross-cultural dialogue, debate, and—of necessity—critique.

A concept that may serve the purpose of conveying the role of shared human values asserted in claims 9 and 10 better than do

13. *The Crooked Timber of Humanity* (New York: Alfred A. Knopf, 1991), 14, 18.

those of normality or humanity is that of "the human condition." This concept has been made to stand for much that human beings have been thought to share, from a "fallen" state to descent from or creation by a variety of gods, to biological predetermination. But seen from a minimalist point of view, it connotes at the very least the survival needs that human beings share with one another and with other species: the fact that they will expire if they do not receive enough oxygen, nourishment, water, and shelter from the elements.[14] It is in response to these survival needs that human beings have joined together in communities, and in turn have had to work out at least basic forms of mutual support, respect, and forbearance. On such a common basis, extraordinary variation has been possible. As Samuel Johnson observed, "Yet amidst all the disorder and inequality which variety of discipline, example, conversation, and employment produce in the intellectual advances of different men, there is still discovered by a vigilant spectator such a general and remote similitude as may be expected in the same common nature affected by external circumstances indefinitely varied."[15]

A minimalist interpretation of "the human condition" can draw on Johnson's view to reduce the tension between the two passages cited at the beginning of this chapter. It addresses our experience as human beings who, sharing "the same common nature" at least from the point of view of our survival needs, yet also "affected by external circumstances indefinitely varied," do in fact most often acknowledge at least a minimum of basic human values. In turn, such an interpretation may help us to conceive of at least limited common ground for moral debate and for the critique of clearly inhumane practices that Berlin wishes to retain no matter how pluralist his view of ethics.

Can such a minimalist view of values offering common ground for dialogue, debate, and critique make a genuine difference in practice? Many have their doubts on this score, even if they accept the

14. See Bernard Williams, *Ethics and the Limits of Philosophy* (Cambridge: Harvard University Press, 1985), 152–53, for a view of the human condition as based on human needs.

15. *The Rambler* (1750; New York: Dutton, Everyman's Library, 1957), 151.

argument for such a view in principle. Still others regard it as confusing and possibly counterproductive to take moral considerations into account in policy making. Thinkers in both groups regard it as utopian to seek to go against human nature, given the predisposition to violence and lawlessness they see as making the recurrence of war inevitable. At the end of a century as violent as ours, with adversaries the world over possessing technological means that render the alternative to seeking common ground for cross-cultural collaboration more dismal than ever, it is worth reexamining that charge of utopianism.

Chapter 4

Advocates of Lasting Peace
Utopians or Realists?

The plans that Erasmus, the Abbé de Saint-Pierre, Kant, and others offered for moving toward a universal and perpetual peace have long been dismissed as utopian or hypocritical, at times even suppressed as dangerously heretical. These thinkers challenged the common perception of war as an immutable aspect of the human condition and of the idea of lasting peace as possible, if at all, only in the hereafter—a perception that has seemed self-evident to most commentators from antiquity onward, whether they espouse what has come to be called a realist, a pacifist, or a just-war perspective.

In the nuclear age, however, nations can no longer afford to leave that perception unchallenged. They cannot run the risk of yet another great war; even in the unlikely event that such a war could be kept nonnuclear, today's conventional weapons would bring devastation beyond anything that humanity has experienced. Likewise, prolonged regional conflicts are increasingly seen as intolerable, given the levels of impoverishment, homelessness, and suffering that they inflict as well as the risk that they will ignite large-scale war. The social and environmental threats that nations now face collectively, moreover, call for levels of cooperation that will be unattainable except under conditions of lasting peace.

If, therefore, self-preservation now dictates collective efforts toward a lasting world peace, no matter how difficult to achieve, it is worth reexamining the writings of those who once pioneered such an approach. To be sure, they had more than their share of quick-fix solutions; and the particulars of even the most sophisticated of their plans can hardly be adequate for today's international relations. But two aspects of the best among their writings are as relevant today as in the past: their intrepid challenges to the common assumption that war will always be with us; and their suggestions for how to create a social climate conducive to the forging of a stable peace.

In the works of Desiderius Erasmus and Immanuel Kant, these lines of reasoning are pursued with special subtlety and force. They are as relevant to practical choice by contemporary governments, organizations, and individuals as to theories of war and peace. By now, many proponents of realist, just-war, and pacifist theories have come to agree on the necessity of working toward the goal of lasting peace, while continuing to differ about the means. It will help, in debating the means, to consider the coordinated, practical measures explored by these two thinkers in the light of all that we have later learned about which ones work best and why. In turn, such a study will require a rethinking, from within each of the three theoretical perspectives, of the role and the demands of morality in international relations.

Human Nature, War, and Ethics

It will be enough for me, however, if these words of mine are judged useful by those who want to understand clearly the events which took place in the past and which (human nature being what it is) will, at some time or other and in much the same ways, be repeated in the future.

Thucydides, *The Peloponnesian Wars*

The conflict between Athens and Sparta depicted by Thucydides has been reenacted time and again over the centuries. Most thinkers since his time, whether they have gloried in war, tolerated it, or denounced it, have taken for granted that it will remain a constant in the human condition. To be sure, they have argued, it can be staved off for a time or fenced away from one or more regions of the world; but experience shows that it cannot be eradicated for good. To think otherwise is to be caught in an illusion.

They have explained the perennial nature of war by referring, as did Thucydides in the passage cited above, to human nature: to incorrigible traits such as pugnacity, vindictiveness, partisanship, and the lust for conquest and power; but they have also invoked, as did he, the external circumstances of scarcity and hardship that drive communities to fight one another in order to survive. These traits and circumstances have in turn often been seen as inflicted on human beings by fate or some supernatural power. Thus, Homer portrays the gods as prolonging the Trojan War by using participants for purposes of sport or intrigue or amusement; and the biblical God has been interpreted as imposing hardship and tribulation to punish human beings, to test them, or to separate the just from the unjust.

The debate about how to respond to such a predicament was, for centuries, largely three-cornered. Against the common background of war as a constant in the human condition, the responses accorded with one or the other of what we now call the realist, pacifist, and just-war traditions—though with all the overlays, interlacings, and variations that would naturally accrue over the centuries.

Realists, often invoking Thucydides, held that it was useless and perhaps even dangerous to rail against the cruelty and immorality of anything as perennial as war; what mattered, rather, was to act according to the best available strategic estimates of what would serve a ruler's or nation's self-interest. In this way, engaging in wars for the sake of preserving or increasing a nation's independence, wealth, or power was acceptable, even commendable. Moral judgments about the rights and wrongs committed in starting any particular war or in its conduct were, according to such a view, beside the point.

Tertullian, Origen, and other early Christian pacifists argued, on the contrary, that morality and religion commanded human beings to renounce war and all killing. No matter how prevalent war might be and no matter what interests any one war might serve, the Christian's duty was to refuse all participation. Otherwise the biblical injunction to love one's enemy and to turn the other cheek would lose all meaning.

Just-war theorists, from Augustine and Thomas Aquinas on, advocated, on similarly religious and moral grounds, limiting rather than renouncing the recourse to war. Among the causes these thinkers regarded as justifying going to war were, variously, wars fought in self-defense, wars in defense of an ally, wars to punish wrongdoing, and wars to convert unbelievers. But justice also required careful scrutiny of the conduct of warring forces, no matter how just the cause to which they laid claim.

Beginning with the sixteenth century, a fourth pattern emerged among the responses to the prevalence of war—that of Erasmus and other advocates of specific, practical steps toward what they called "perpetual peace." They challenged not only the commonly accepted thesis regarding war's perennial nature, but also the specific claims of thinkers in the existing three traditions regarding when, if ever, war was legitimate. Because the proposals for a lasting peace were often summarily dismissed or even suppressed, they did not constitute a lineage of well-known fundamental texts, nor give rise to the wealth of commentary generated by the other traditions. As a result, advocates of perpetual peace were rarely seen as contributing to a tradition separate from that of pacifism. By now, however, it is becoming increasingly clear that they were shaping a new tradition of thinking about war and peace fully as worthy of study as the three others. To this tradition belong, among others, Desiderius Erasmus, William Penn, the Abbé de Saint-Pierre, Immanuel Kant, and Jeremy Bentham. Among its interpreters and critics are Leibniz, Rousseau, and Hegel.[1]

---

1. For the works by Erasmus that contributed most to this tradition, see notes 2, 4, and 6 below. See also Edwin D. Mead, ed., *The Great Design of Henry IV from the Memoirs of the Duke of Sully* (1559–1641; Boston: Ginn and Co., 1909); William Penn, "An Essay Towards the Present and Future Peace of Europe" (1693), in Fredrick B. Tolles and E. Gordon Alderfer, eds., *The Witness of William Penn* (New York: Macmillan and Co., 1957), 140–59; Abbé de Saint-Pierre, *Selections from the 2nd Edition of the Abrégé du Projet de Paix Perpétuelle* (1712; London: Sweet and Maxwell, 1927); Immanuel Kant, "Perpetual Peace: A Philosophical Sketch" (1795), in Hans Reiss, ed., *Kant's Political Writings* (Cambridge: Cambridge University Press, 1970), 93–130; Jeremy Bentham, "Essay on Universal Peace. Essay IV. A Plan for a Universal and Perpetual Peace" (1789, first published in 1843), in Charles W. Everett, ed., *Jeremy Bentham* (London: Weidenfeld and Nicolson, 1966), 195–229; Gottfried Wilhelm Leibniz, "Observation sur le projet d'une paix perpétuelle de M. l'abbé de St. Pierre," in L. Dutens, ed., *Opera*

Thinkers in this fourth tradition had no illusions that peace was somehow a natural state for the human species. They could hardly quarrel with the historical record of recurrent aggression, injustice, and warfare. They meant, rather, to challenge what they saw as the unthinking extrapolation from that past experience to the future: the unwarranted inference from what has been to what must always be. Over time, they argued, nations could break away from the destructive patterns of the past. But they had little faith, unlike a number of utopians, in some convulsive political or religious transformation that would bring permanent harmony—the more so as they had seen at close hand the corrupting and brutalizing effects of unrestrained violence on behalf of such causes, both on perpetrators and on victims, no matter how humane the original motives.

The synthesis arrived at by these thinkers was eloquently voiced by Erasmus and formulated with greater precision, clarity, and scope by Kant. It employs both the realist language of strategy and the normative language common to pacifists and just-war theorists. According to this view, nations can achieve lasting strategic benefits by only respecting fundamental moral constraints; but it does little good merely to stress these constraints without setting forth concerted, practical steps to facilitate and reinforce their observance. War may indeed continue to be our lot, they admit; but we are free to choose differently. Each generation, far from being condemned to reenact the errors of the past, has the opportunity to learn from the mistakes and disasters of previous generations, and thus the capacity to move, over time, toward a state of perpetual peace.

Erasmus

> *What is more brittle than the life of man? How short its natural duration! How liable to disease, how exposed to momentary*

Omnia (Geneva, 1768), vol. 5; Jean-Jacques Rousseau (editing and commenting upon the work of the Abbé de Saint-Pierre), *A Project of Perpetual Peace* (1782), trans. Edith M. Nuttall (London: Richard Cobden-Sanderson, 1927); Friedrich Hegel, *Philosophy of Right* (1821), trans. T. M. Knox (Oxford: Clarendon Press, 1958), 208–16.

accidents! Yet though natural and inevitable evils are more than
can be borne with patience, man, fool that he is, brings the greatest
and worst calamities upon his own head. . . . To arms he rushes
at all times and in all places; no bounds to his fury, no end to his
destructive vengeance.

Erasmus, The Complaint of Peace

Few have spoken out more forcefully than Erasmus about the
folly and cruelty of war. Already in his *Adages,* published in 1500
and reportedly more widely circulated at the time than any other
book save the Bible, he had inveighed against war in an essay
entitled *"Dulce Bellum Inexpertis"* or "War Is Sweet to Those Who
Have Not Experienced It."[2] Between 1514 and 1517, when a brief
interval in the near-constant wars between European powers made
a more lasting peace seem at least possible, Erasmus devoted himself
wholeheartedly to helping bring it about.[3] He suggested summon-
ing a "congress of kings"—a "summit meeting" among the kings
of Europe—for the purpose of signing an indissoluble peace agreement. He revised and expanded his essay on the sweetness of war
to the inexperienced for the latest edition of the *Adages.* And he
wrote a manual for princes—*The Education of the Christian Prince*—
to guide the young Prince Charles of Spain, who was shortly to
become Charles V.[4]

This book presents a striking contrast to Machiavelli's *Prince*
(written a few years earlier but still unpublished). Where Machiavelli had broken away from the stress on virtues so common in
previous books of advice for princes, and urged the prince to resort

2. A later edition of *The Adages,* published in 1515, contained a greatly expanded
version of *"Dulce Bellum Inexpertis."* See Margaret Mann Phillips, ed., *The Adages
of Erasmus: A Study with Interpretations* (Cambridge: Cambridge University Press,
1964), 308–53.
3. In 1516, France and Switzerland concluded the Treaty of Fribourg, known as
"La paix perpétuelle," which lasted until the French Revolution. The year before,
Henry VIII had concluded a "permanent" but much more short-lived peace with
France. For a few years, nevertheless, Erasmus, Thomas More, and other humanists
had hopes for a flowering of peace that would permit the shaping of a new political
and cultural order.
4. *The Education of a Christian Prince* (1516), trans. Lester K. Born (New York:
Octagon Books, 1973).

to violence, deceit, and betrayal whenever necessary to gain or retain power, Erasmus emphasized moral virtues as prerequisites to a good reign. And whereas Machiavelli had urged the prince to study war above all else, Erasmus gave precedence to learning "the arts of peace": how to establish and preserve a rule of just laws, improve the public's health, ensure an adequate food supply, beautify cities and their surroundings, and master the diplomatic alternatives to war. A last, brief chapter, entitled "On Beginning War," counsels the prince never to go to war at all, save as a last resort; but "if so ruinous an occurrence cannot be avoided," then the prince should wage it with a minimum of bloodshed and conclude the struggle as soon as possible.[5]

A year after publishing his *Education,* Erasmus returned to the charge with *The Complaint of Peace.*[6] This time, Erasmus sent his book to all the rulers of Europe rather than addressing it to one prince alone. Peace, speaking "in her own person, rejected from all countries," is the protagonist of this book. Her complaint addresses the irrationality and inhumanity of war. Of all the evils that beset humanity, she argues, surely war is the most puzzling, because it is self-chosen. If the insults and indignities heaped upon her went along with advantages to mortals, she could at least understand why they might persecute her. Yet, since mortals unleash a deluge of calamities upon themselves through engaging in war, she has to speak to them of their misfortune even more than complain of her own.

In these several works, Erasmus gives short shrift to the realist and just-war schools of thinking that ruled the day at the courts of Spain and other European powers; at the same time he distances himself from pacifist claims to nonresistance at all times. However

---

5. Ibid., 249.
6. *The Complaint of Peace* (1517; Boston: Charles Williams, 1813). For a more recent translation, though not entirely complete, see "Peace Protests!" in Jose Chapiro, trans., *Erasmus and Our Struggle for Peace* (Boston: Beacon Press, 1950), 131–84. In a letter from 1523 Erasmus comments bitterly to a friend that he must "soon compose the Epitaph, rather than the Complaint, of Peace, as she seems to be dead and buried and not very likely to revive" (cited in translator's preface, 1813 edition of *Complaint of Peace,* iv).

attractive a war may seem at the outset, first of all, he argues, it appeals to dreamers, not to realists. From war "comes the shipwreck of all that is good and from it the sea of all calamities."[7] Claims to the benefits of war result, he claims, from inexperience. Those who have had to live through war are too rarely consulted; as a result, each generation foolishly undertakes to learn about war's costs from scratch. Even on the strictest strategic grounds of national self-interest, Erasmus insists, a truly realistic look at the costs of war should dissuade a prince from just about all recourse to arms.

Second, Erasmus evinces equal skepticism about claims that particular crusades and wars are just ones. He writes scornfully of the spectacle of clergy on both sides of so many wars declaiming the just cause of their own rulers. Who does not think his own cause just, he asks, warning that the likelihood of bias and corruption is so great in seeking reasons for going to war that "the good Christian Prince should hold under suspicion every war, no matter how just." This suspicion, he held, was the more necessary, since so many conquests and crusades were being fought in the name of the Christian Church, even though "the whole philosophy of Christ teaches against it."[8]

Third, Erasmus addresses pacifist concerns by holding that wars in self-defense are, indeed, legitimate, but only after all other alternatives, including arbitration, have been exhausted; and only after obtaining the consent of the people, who will, after all, suffer so much more directly from any war than their rulers. If such procedures were taken seriously, it is doubtful whether any war would remain to be fought: but the decision to avoid going to war would then be made on pragmatic as well as on religious and moral grounds, rather than constituting an absolutist rejection of all war no matter what the costs.

In *The Complaint of Peace,* Erasmus advances a carefully reasoned attack on the underlying assumption widely shared in his day as in our own: that violent conflict and organized war are somehow inherent in the human condition. He discusses each of the three

7. *Education,* 249.
8. Ibid., 250, 251.

most common explanations for why human existence should be so burdened with the ravages and deaths that war brings: that war will always be with us because of indelible deficiencies in human nature, unrelenting outside pressures, or divine intention—perhaps because of all three.

To those who embrace the first explanation and point to greed, aggressiveness, and vindictiveness as human traits so pervasive that they eliminate all chances of a lasting peace, Erasmus responds by asking: What is it in human beings that predisposes them to war? Are they saddled with indelible personality traits that preclude all chances of a lasting peace? How do we have to envisage human nature for this to be true? If it carries with it traits that make wars inevitable, Erasmus begins, they cannot be traits shared with animals, since animals show no organized hostility to members of their own species. The conduct of human beings can be so much baser than that of animals that the word *bestiality* bestowed upon the worst forms of human conduct is unfair to animals.[9] Neither the viciousness that human beings can show one another nor the increasingly destructive machinery they were coming to employ in combat had equivalents elsewhere in nature.

What about the traits that distinguish persons from animals? Surely they are not such as to predispose us to war. Our human capacity to reason, our inability to survive alone that makes us dependent on family and society, and our "power of speech, the most conciliating instrument of social connection and cordial love"— these traits, Erasmus argues, need hardly be conducive to war. On the contrary, they should predispose human beings to living with one another in peace, not war, he concludes. It is only our familiarity

9. Comparisons between animals and human beings traditionally placed humans above animals in the chain of being. Cicero, among many others, had argued that the two ways of doing wrong—by force or by fraud—were both bestial: "Fraud seems to belong to the cunning fox, force to the lion: both are wholly unworthy of man, but fraud is the more contemptible" *(De Officiis [Of Duties]* [44 B.C.], I, XIII). Machiavelli had accepted the comparison only to argue that human beings ought to learn from the fox and the lion in those respects. Erasmus intended to show, on the contrary, that force and fraud on the scale practiced by humans and with the means at their disposal were of an entirely different order, and that to attribute such aspects of human conduct to animals was merely to calumny them.

with "everlasting feuds, litigation, and murder" that produces the conduct that we mistake for a natural predisposition to war—the more readily so if leadership, education, and social reforms offer no counterbalance.

To the second standard explanation—that outside pressures of scarcity and hardship and natural calamities inevitably cause recurrent conflicts—Erasmus answers that it is surely madness to add to these undoubted outside pressures all the suffering that wars bring. The corruption into which human societies have fallen has rendered them unable to deal in the most reasonable way with conflicts engendered by such hardships. For the state of affairs in his own period, Erasmus holds rulers responsible above all others. In their greed and folly, they repeatedly and mindlessly drag their peoples into the tragedy of war. But rulers cannot wreak this havoc by themselves. Hatred and conflict have become endemic. Erasmus catalogs the groups that harbor such traits: citizens given to strife and dissension; courtiers poisoning the climate with their intrigues and grudges; scholars and theologians at daggerheads with one another; clergy and monastics tearing one another to pieces through partisan disputes; mercenary soldiers feeding as vermin on the miseries they inflict on human communities.

The third explanation common since antiquity—that the human predisposition to war is due to divine intention—could in principle account for the first two and undercut all proposals for reform. While human nature may not by itself be destined for perennial warfare and while outside pressures might not of their own precipitate it, God may have seen to it that these conditions would nevertheless persist. In response to such theological claims, Erasmus invokes Scripture: Christ's central message, quite to the contrary, is one of peace, forgiveness, and nonviolence. If anyone intended the brutal, near-constant warfare that admittedly beset Europe in his time, he suggested, it must rather be Satan.

Having countered the three explanations most often brought forth to buttress ancient dogmas about the inevitability of war, Erasmus turns to the future. Though a lasting peace is possible, great changes are needed to bring it about. Peace cannot simply be ordained by religious or political authorities, nor can it be mandated merely through treaties and alliances alone. Rather, it has to be undertaken at every level of society. Kings must work together for the good of their citizens and consult them before embarking on any war. And citizens must grant kings "just so many privileges and prerogatives as are for the public good and no more."[10] Erasmus, who never ceased criticizing kings for their exploitative and brutal scheming at the expense of their peoples, here hints at the alternative of government limited by democratic consent—hard to envisage in his time and dangerous for anyone to promote. If nations submitted, further, to an international court of arbitration, they could avert many wars; if need be, peace should be purchased to prevent still others.

Bishops and priests must likewise unite against war and cease appealing to just-war theory to excuse every war their king or the Pope undertakes. The nobility and all magistrates must also collaborate in the work of peace. To each of these groups, and to "all who call themselves Christians," Erasmus pleads: "unite with one heart and one soul, in the abolition of war, and the establishment of perpetual and universal peace."[11] But beyond Christianity, Erasmus also wishes to suggest that the hostilities between faiths and nationalities could be tempered if only people reflected that they are, above all, members of the same human race, sharing the most basic survival needs and values: "If name of country is of such nature as to create bonds between those who have a common country, why do not men resolve that the universe should become the country of all?"[12]

During the remaining decades of his life, Erasmus saw the world move relentlessly in the opposite direction. Wars of conquest succeeded one another, religious and ideological persecution spread, and the religious conflicts that would later culminate in the Thirty Years' War intensified. Though frequently reprinted, Erasmus's writings on war and peace fell out of favor in many

---

10. *Complaint of Peace*, 51.
11. Ibid., 79.
12. "Peace Protests!" 173.

quarters. Many were burned and prohibited as heretical during the Counter-Reformation.[13] To militants of every persuasion, his insistence on arbitration and on other peaceful means of resolving conflicts seemed an endorsement of cowardice and vacillation. Over time, his work was deprecated, at times outlawed. As a result, later advocates of perpetual peace too often ignored the depth and scope of his proposals. They tended, rather, to stress purely diplomatic methods for achieving lasting peace. Thus the Abbé de Saint-Pierre proposed, in 1712, a permanent league of European rulers under common laws.[14] Even today, most texts dealing with issues of war and peace mention Erasmus only in passing if at all.

Kant

> *Wars, tense and unremitting military preparations, and the resultant distress which every state must eventually feel within itself, even in the midst of peace—these are the means by which nature drives nations to make initially imperfect attempts, but finally, after many devastations, upheavals, and even complete inner exhaustion of their powers, to take the step which reason could have suggested to them even without so many sad experiences—that of abandoning a lawless state of nature and entering a federation of peoples in which every state, even the smallest, could expect to derive its security and rights.*
>
> Immanuel Kant, "Idea for a Universal History with a
> Cosmopolitan Purpose"

It was not until Kant published his essay on "Perpetual Peace" in 1795, building on earlier works such as his article on "Universal History," that individual and institutional change was once

---

13. See Marcel Battaillon, *Erasme et L'Espagne* (Paris: Librairie E. Droz, 1937), 2:29.
14. *Selections from the Abrégé du Projet de Paix Perpétuelle.* See also Rousseau, *A Project of Perpetual Peace.*

again brought into public debate as a necessary prerequisite for arriving at a lasting peace.[15] Like Erasmus, Kant argues that such a state of peace is fully achievable, even though war, thus far, has been a constant factor in the human condition. But Kant sees greater obstacles to achieving such a peace than Erasmus ever conceded.

Kant shares, first of all, the Hobbesian view of international relations as anarchic: nations exist in a "lawless state of nature" where "the depravity of human nature is displayed without disguise," whereas within civil societies, it is at least controlled by governmental constraints.[16] Unlike Erasmus, Kant had long agreed with those who held that wars had served important purposes throughout history and had most likely even been intended for such purposes by nature. Without the incentives provided by competition, lust for power, and conflict, human beings might never have developed their talents or their technology much beyond the animal stage. But wars had become increasingly destructive and risked becoming even more so, to the point where a war of extermination could bring about "perpetual peace only on the vast graveyard of the human race."[17] As a result, the time had come when nations would have to break out of the state of nature or perish.

Given Kant's concessions to the holders of the majority thesis, how did he envisage that such a change might be brought about? To begin with, he saw grounds for hope that nature had intended such a shift for human beings. We cannot prove that this is so, nor even infer it; but it is "more than an empty chimera."[18] Each individual life is brief and flawed; but through the transmission of experience, human beings may, in the end, achieve a sufficient degree of rationality and the capacity to cooperate in achieving security for themselves and their descendants. And that it is *possible* for human beings, thus equipped, to change is clear; for although

15. "Perpetual Peace" (1795) and "Idea for a Universal History with a Cosmopolitan Purpose" (1784), in Reiss, ed., *Kant's Political Writings*, 93–130, 41–53.
16. "Perpetual Peace," 103.
17. Ibid., 96.
18. Ibid., 114.

Kant acknowledges that human beings do exhibit a propensity to evil and to war, they also possess a predisposition to good. They are at all times free to choose to act according to what they recognize as right and to guide their lives differently. Though peace will not come of its own accord nor from an oversupply of human goodness, it can be instituted, chosen.

But bringing peace about will require far more than the piecemeal reforms too often advocated. Plans such as those of the Abbé de Saint-Pierre have been ridiculed as wild and fanciful, Kant suggests, in part because their proponents take for granted that the necessary changes are imminent, easy to institute, and unproblematic. Any realistic approach would have to be based on the recognition, on the contrary, that change would be slow to come, that it would require reforms at every level of national and international society, and that such reforms would be bound to fail over and over again unless measures were first taken to change the very atmosphere in which negotiations are carried out.

Accordingly, Kant begins, in "Perpetual Peace," by proposing a set of "preliminary articles" to help prepare the social climate for the larger institutional reforms. Some of these preliminary articles set forth steps that governments could take right away to reduce the distrust standing in the way of all meaningful cooperation. If governments could negotiate peace agreements without secret reservations concerning future wars, if they could abstain from forcible interference in the affairs of other nations, and if they could, even when at war, discontinue what he called "dishonorable stratagems," such as the breach of agreements or treaties, the employment of assassins, and the instigation of treason within one another's states, then they would, at the very least, not be poisoning the atmosphere for peace negotiations.[19]

By stressing basic moral constraints, not only within but also between nations—constraints on violence, deceit, breaches of faith, and excessive secrecy—Kant does not mean to say that these constraints, by themselves, will provide all that is needed to ensure

19. Ibid., 96.

a lasting peace.[20] He merely insists that so long as they are not taken into account, there can be no chance whatsoever of instituting such a peace. Distrust, as Hobbes had pointed out before him, undermines the incentive to cooperate. Little wonder, then, Kant argues, that a lasting peace has been out of reach: the *reasons* for such debilitating distrust have never been carefully addressed. But at the same time, we need not imagine that peace will continue to elude humankind, once the constraints are taken seriously and once it becomes clear that they are indispensable to long-term collective survival.

Along with creating a climate that allows for institutional reform, Kant sees three "definite articles" as necessary for a perpetual peace among nations. The first calls for the achievement, over time, of a world in which more and more states have representative governments elected by free citizens equal before the law. Such a form of government will do much to cut back on the wars of any state, since citizens tend to be far less enthusiastic about wars they know they will have to pay for and fight in than autocratic leaders who impose taxes and give orders from the sidelines. But of course, citizens in such states can still be persuaded to concur in wars of conquest by skillful propaganda; as a result, additional international measures are necessary. The second article proposed by Kant calls for the joining together of states in a federation capable of keeping a just peace; and the third for respecting the human rights of visitors or outsiders to such states so as, for example, not to enslave them or conquer them.

Kant may well have been thought utopian to speak of the spread and federating of representative governments as conducive to lasting peace in 1795, when only the young American republic could lay claim to a stable form of such governance, and to invoke "a universal right of humanity" in condemning slavery and imperialistic conquest in a period when these practices were so widespread. But he insisted that such an idea was not "fantastic and overstrained":

---

20. For a discussion of these constraints in Kant's writings and of their role in international relations, see Sissela Bok, *A Strategy for Peace: Human Values and the Threat of War* (New York: Pantheon Books, 1989).

"Only under this condition can we flatter ourselves that we are continually advancing toward a perpetual peace."[21]

The Prospects for Perpetual Peace in the Nuclear Era

In your hands rests our future. By your labors at this conference we shall know if suffering humanity is to achieve a just and lasting peace.

President Harry S. Truman, speaking to delegates
at the opening session of the U. N. Conference in
San Francisco, April 23, 1945.

In 1953, President Dwight D. Eisenhower spoke of the change that the Cold War had brought since "that hopeful spring of 1945." At that time, "The hope of all just men . . . was for a just and lasting peace. The eight years that have passed have seen that hope waver, grow dim, and almost die. And the shadow of fear again has darkly lengthened across the world."[22]

For three and a half decades after Eisenhower's address, the shadow of fear continued to lengthen. The great powers built up vast stockpiles of nuclear weapons with unprecedented destructive potential, and still more nations stood poised to follow suit. Kant's warning that a war of extermination could bring perpetual peace on the vast graveyard of humanity took on a directness in the nuclear age over the decades that even he could hardly have predicted.

The full horror of such a prospect shifted the incentives with respect to war decisively. It became a commonplace for world leaders to speak of the necessity of bringing about a lasting peace and of making every effort to avoid unleashing, even accidentally, another major war. A similar realignment took place within the three

21. "Perpetual Peace," 108.
22. "The Chance for Peace," address delivered before the American Society of Newspaper Editors, April 16, 1953. Reprinted in Kenneth E. Alrutz et al., eds., *War and Peace*, Lynchburg College Symposium Readings, vol. 5 (Lanham, Md.: University Press of America, 1982), 621.

major traditions of thinking about war and peace. Realists, just-war theorists, and pacifists moved closer to one another, and in turn—often without knowing it—to the principled yet practical stance by which thinkers in the perpetual-peace tradition combined moral and strategic considerations.

Already during the nineteenth century, many pacifists were adopting the language of the perpetual-peace tradition, its stress on step-by-step efforts to strengthen conditions for lasting peace, and its support for international organizations. Thus, British Quakers founded a "Society for the Promotion of Permanent and Universal Peace" in 1816.[23] They disagreed among themselves, as did other pacifists, about whether to endorse complete nonresistance in all wars or to accept resistance in clear cases of self-defense when all other methods have failed. This disagreement still persists among pacifists today. Many who, like Tolstoy, were once in favor of unilateral disarmament and noncooperation with all military activities, including strictly defensive ones, have had to weigh whether such a stance with respect to nuclear weapons might not increase, rather than decrease, the risks to humanity. "Do what is right though the earth should perish" has taken on an entirely new and more literal meaning since Hiroshima and Nagasaki.[24]

Only a minority of those active in contemporary peace movements adopted such an absolutist stance. But whether or not they did, the threat to collective survival posed by nuclear weapons induced many to focus their attention sharply on weapons systems and government military strategy. Their research and advocacy at times reflected back, as in a mirror, the priorities of their opponents, and the underlying moral debate came to center on issues of violence and nonviolence. But with the end of the Cold War

23. See F. H. Hinsley, *Power and the Pursuit of Peace* (Cambridge: Cambridge University Press, 1963), 93–97.

24. Kant explicitly defended this motto, but while it committed him to absolutism with respect to lying, it did not do so when it came to violence, since he regarded violence in self-defense as legitimate. See Sissela Bok, "Kant's Arguments in Support of the Maxim 'Do What Is Right Though the World Should Perish,'" *Argumentation* 2 (1988): 7–25, reprinted in David M. Rosenthal and Fadlou Shehadi, eds., *Applied Ethics and Ethical Theology* (Salt Lake City: University of Utah Press, 1988), 191–212.

it became clear that the chances for lasting peace depended on a complex linkage of individual, domestic, and international policies and that a more comprehensive moral framework was needed, in which nonviolence would play a central but not exclusive role. In the Philippines, in East Germany, in Czechoslovakia, and in Hungary, "people power" has shown itself victorious in the face of massively armed governments: as Václav Havel long continued to insist at great personal risk, citizens who are striving to "live within the truth" can overthrow dictatorships by nonviolent means.[25]

Realists, whether of a practical or a theoretical bent, have also been increasingly driven to reconsider their most fundamental presumptions in the face of the nuclear predicament. Many among them once argued that strict national self-interest should dictate foreign policy, quite apart from what might be desirable for other nations, and that morality was beside the point in international relations. By now, the first argument has had to be sharply modified and the second abandoned. First, national self-interest now clearly mandates a concern for comprehensive international security; international security, in turn, is affected by such factors as hunger, deforestation, regional strife, and population growth the world over. Even from a strictly strategic point of view, therefore, it matters to attend to these factors.

Second, doing so necessitates being alert to the role of moral claims such as those regarding fundamental human rights. References to human rights abroad were once dismissed by many realists as sentimental, given political realities in most nations, and as potentially counterproductive efforts to interfere with sovereign states. But the political power of calls for human rights can no longer be denied, nor their importance to foreign relations. The same is true with respect to the action or inaction on the part of governments in matters of environmental or nuclear strategy. It is not surprising, therefore, that George Kennan, who has long argued against the assumption "that state behavior is a fit subject for moral judgment,"

25. "The Power of the Powerless," in Václav Havel et al., *The Power of the Powerless: Citizens against the State in Central-Eastern Europe* (London: Hutchinson, 1985), 39.

does not hesitate to express such moral judgments when it comes to nuclear weapons. In *The Nuclear Delusion*, he cries out, in a tone that Erasmus would not have disowned, against the readiness to use nuclear weapons against other human beings, thus placing in jeopardy all of civilization, calling it a blasphemy and "an indignity of monstrous proportions."[26]

Contemporary just-war theorists, unlike those in the realist tradition, have consistently advanced moral claims in the context of war and peace. If the nuclear balance of terror accelerated a shift, on their part, in the direction of Erasmus and Kant, it was in reducing the range of wars seen as potentially just ones. It became harder to view many wars as likely to serve the cause of justice. Whereas Augustine and Thomas Aquinas argued in favor of certain wars to avenge wrongs, the U.S. Catholic Bishops stated, in 1983, that "if war of retribution was ever justifiable, the risks of modern war negate such a claim today." They restated the just-war position so as to exclude, in the contemporary world, nearly all wars as unjust except those of strict self-defense or defense of others under attack, and only then as a last resort. And, like Erasmus and Kant, they emphasized the monumental injustice of governments in channeling such a vast proportion of the world's scarce resources into armaments, calling it "an act of aggression upon the poor."[27]

Marxists also came to narrow the very different criteria that V. I. Lenin and Mao Zedong had elaborated for ascertaining when wars were just. Lenin held that wars against oppressors by wage earners and enslaved or colonized peoples were fully legitimate, progressive, and necessary: "Whosoever wants a lasting and democratic peace must stand for civil war against the government and the bourgeoisie."[28] Mao likewise argued that the only just wars are

---

26. *The Nuclear Delusion* (New York: Pantheon Books, 1982).

27. National Council of Catholic Bishops, *The Challenge of Peace: God's Promise and Our Response* (Washington, D.C.: Office of Publishing Services, U.S.C.C., 1983), 39, v. For a secular interpretation of just-war doctrine that similarly restricts the causes for just war, see Robert W. Tucker, *The Just War: A Study in Contemporary American Doctrine* (Baltimore: Johns Hopkins University Press, 1960).

28. "The Question of Peace" (1915), in *Collected Works* (Moscow: Progress Publishers, 1968), 91:290–94, 297–338; see also "Socialism and War" (1915), 91:297–338, and "April Theses, 1917," 24:21–26.

nonpredatory wars, wars of liberation. "Communists will support every just and non-predatory war for liberation, and they will stand in the forefront of the struggle."[29] It became increasingly difficult, however, to maintain that the fanning of regional wars had, in fact, promoted justice; and the faith that a lasting peace was bound to result from such warfare faltered even among many committed Marxists. Similarly, Marx's castigation of moral claims—concerning justice and rights, in particular—as "ideological nonsense" has undergone impassioned rejection throughout much of the past and present communist world.[30]

In the light of all these shifts, Kant's essay on "Perpetual Peace" bears rereading. Nearly two centuries after its publication, it no longer seems overstrained or utopian to link the chances for peace with the respect for human rights and with the growing cooperation between nations in which those rights are protected by representative forms of government. And just as contemporary thinkers, who once rejected fundamental moral claims as irrelevant or postponed them as premature, have been led to take them into consideration on strict realist grounds, so, too, have many who once based their position on strictly normative claims had to acknowledge that strategic realities affect their choices. To be sure, the goal of lasting peace still seems not only out of reach but also threatened, in ways not fully understood even in the early 1990s, by the growth of ethnic strife and humanitarian crises. What remains clear, however, is that it no longer makes either strategic or moral sense for governments, policy advisers, or theorists not to try to move in the direction of that goal.

But if so many have come to take such a goal seriously as at least worth striving for, however utopian it seemed when first advocated by thinkers in the perpetual-peace tradition, then there is reason to take equally seriously the ways of moving closer to that goal that these thinkers suggested. True, they could not have foreseen the

29. M. Rejai, ed., *Mao Tse-tung: On Revolution and War* (Garden City: Doubleday, 1970), 67.

30. D. McLellan, ed., *Karl Marx: Selected Writings* (Oxford: Oxford University Press, 1977), 568–69.

kinds of negotiations required by today's weapons and international alignments, nor the present social and environmental threats to humanity. These developments call for responses of a complexity that no one could have predicted centuries ago. But the tradition of perpetual peace may be more helpful when it comes to exploring the crucial role of the social climate that determines whether or not adequate levels of cooperation will be possible, and to asking how to strengthen and build on the framework of moral constraints needed at every level of society to keep that climate from deteriorating.

Our century has seen the development of new strategies for bringing about change in ways that respect the social climate. The tradition of nonviolent resistance to oppression that began with Mohandas Gandhi in India and continued with the civil rights struggle led by Martin Luther King, Jr., in the United States has influenced political change in countries as different as South Korea, Chile, and East Germany. Increasingly, we witness a striking contrast. While peaceful transformations have produced astounding successes in one country after another in Eastern Europe, fighting has dragged on almost interminably in Angola, Bosnia, and too many other nations, producing only further suffering. Few have doubted that nonviolent resistance is more respectful of human rights and less likely to brutalize and corrupt its participants. What is becoming ever clearer is that, with the help of modern communications media, such resistance can also bring speedier and more far-reaching results—and that both strategic and moral considerations favor such resistance. Being more protective of the social climate, it is also more conducive to the cooperation that is so desperately needed once the struggle is over.

Nothing guarantees that those who lead such movements to victory will also be able to govern well, or that changes wrought with nonviolent means will not once again succumb to violence. Nor do all efforts at nonviolent resistance succeed, as Tiananmen Square and too many other examples demonstrate. Yet, even when the latter efforts meet with repression, as did the Polish Solidarity struggle for years, nonviolent movements have a better chance of ultimately succeeding than groups that resort to a violent uprising.

Only time will tell whether a cumulative process of nonviolent and principled efforts at domestic and international change can, in the long run, disprove the age-old assumption that war will always be with us. Much that Erasmus, Kant, and others advocated, such as giving citizens a voice with respect to whether or not to undertake a war, convening international parleys and federations, and submitting disputes to arbitration, must have seemed highly improbable—indeed utopian—at the time. But the word *utopia* can have two meanings. One indicates an excellent place or society that is possible but at present merely visionary; the second refers, rather, to an unattainable society advocated by impractical idealists. In arguing that it is possible for human beings to establish a lasting world peace, Erasmus and Kant may well have been utopian in the first sense; but we have everything to lose by not trying to disprove the claim that they were also utopian in the second.

Chapter 5

Humanitarian Emergencies
Whose Rights? Whose Responsibilities?

I refuse to accept the idea that mankind is so tragically bound to the starless midnight of racism and war that the bright daybreak of peace and brotherhood can never become a reality. I refuse to accept the cynical notion that nation after nation must spiral down a militaristic stairway into the hell of the nuclear destruction. I believe that even amid today's mortar bursts and whining bullets, there is still hope for a brighter tomorrow. I believe that wounded justice, lying prostrate on the blood-flowing streets of our nations, can be lifted from this dust of shame to reign supreme among the children of man.

Martin Luther King, Jr., Nobel Peace Prize acceptance
address, December 1964[1]

K ing dared to hope that there would come an end to the violence and injustice perpetrated in cities such as Birmingham, Alabama, and Soweto, in South Africa, and even that the overarching threat to all peoples posed by the nuclear balance of terror could be reversed. By now, however, his words about wounded justice apply to new crises, so numerous and so bitterly entrenched that

---

1. In James M. Washington, ed., *A Testament of Hope: The Essential Writings of Martin Luther King, Jr.* (New York: Harper and Row, 1986), 224–26.

many despair of bringing about a return to peace. The growth in the number and scope of devastating humanitarian emergencies brought about by regional conflicts such as those in Rwanda and Bosnia presents the most immediate, seemingly intractable threat to human security and lasting peace in the post–Cold War era.

At the end of the Cold War, when societies at last could envisage the opportunity to address more energetically the vast long-range challenges that they face collectively, they did not foresee that they would have to divert resources, instead, to escalating humanitarian emergencies. Yet by 1995, the U.N. counted twenty-six such crises, five times as many as were ongoing between 1978 and 1985.[2] The numbers of refugees and of internally displaced persons (who have fled their homes but remain in their homelands) have mounted to levels not seen since World War II. The weaponry available to combatants, often supplied as part of Cold War foreign policy by East and West, places exceptionally large numbers of civilians at risk, including relief workers. In war-torn regions, over 100 million lethal anti-personnel land mines are strewn on fields, along roads, even in cemeteries and school yards, rendering recovery efforts still more dangerous and costly.

Satellite TV brings the resulting suffering into homes the world over with an immediacy never before possible. And the discrepancy between moral rhetoric and human reality grows, as ringing declarations of ever more expansive human rights echo against the daily news flashes of bombardment of civilian "safe havens," of maltreatment and rape, of the toll taken by famine and ethnic cleansing. The reporters and photographers who generate such coverage understandably strive for ever greater realism in presenting the horrors they witness. But the cumulative effect of their coverage has been to flood the media with close-ups of unbearable suffering and, in turn, to widen the gap between guilt-ridden compassion and "compassion fatigue" among the world's publics.

It is no wonder, then, that humanitarian emergencies generate bewilderment among many in the international community about

2. "Global Humanitarian Emergencies, 1995," statement released by the United States Mission to the United Nations (New York: United Nations, 1995), 1.

how to respond. The questions of who should shoulder the responsibility for countering the human rights violations involved and for meeting the survival needs of afflicted populations are only beginning to receive serious debate. So is the ancient question posed most sharply in contemporary guise by these emergencies and faced by some among those who have taken on such a responsibility, often at great personal sacrifice: when do efforts to render assistance risk doing more harm than good? In considering these questions, I shall first discuss certain underlying conceptual and moral aspects of complex emergencies, then take up the practical choices that they raise concerning rights and responsibilities.

The Terms *Complex* and *Emergency*

Part of the bewilderment about how to respond to the growing number of complex emergencies worldwide stems from a failure to sort out and examine the different factual and moral strands of expressions such as *complex emergency* and *humanitarian emergency.* What exactly do they mean? In what sense are certain collective calamities *complex?* How do they differ, once labeled *emergencies,* from equally desperate long-term human predicaments, if at all? These expressions, which were formulated in the early 1990s in the United Nations and have already passed into common parlance among aid organizations and in the media, connote crises in which a number of factors interact to increase conflict, suffering, and destruction. A recent definition holds that "[c]omplex emergencies combine internal conflicts with large-scale displacements of people, mass famine, and fragile or failing economic, political, and social institutions. Some complex emergencies are exacerbated by natural disasters and severely inadequate transport networks."[3]

Definitions of complex emergencies or complex disasters often also include factors such as human rights abuses; psychosocial trauma; dangers attending the work of relief workers, human rights monitors, and peacekeeping forces; ethnic tensions; and

3. Ibid.

deterioration of the physical infrastructure. All attempts to characterize such crises concern, implicitly or explicitly, vast threats to human survival—what one commentator calls "a lethal combination of starvation, economic collapse, civil strife and disintegrating political authority."[4]

The expression *complex emergency* is more, therefore, than a label for today's crises. It points to clusters of causes, of human needs, and of possible remedies. From an immediate practical point of view, the expression offers neutral, nonaccusatory language that may facilitate negotiations with obstructionist governments or warring parties for safe passage or safe havens. Like many similar abstractions, however, *complex emergency* can also function as a euphemism that makes it possible for outsiders to make dispassionate references to unspeakable forms of inhumanity and to human suffering so stark as to be almost unbearable, if truly perceived.

The terms *complex* and *emergency* are themselves highly abstract and multilayered, with many meanings that only partially enter into the concept of "complex emergency." When used together, the two words also take on special moral connotations that they do not otherwise possess. So long as these interlocking meanings and moral connotations are not sorted out, it is easier either to settle for the use of the concept as euphemism or to read into it unexamined moral premises and untested, undebated conclusions about responsibilities, rights, and obligations. It is worth considering each of the two constituent words in turn, therefore, along with *humanitarian*, so often wedged between them, as a background to the larger debate about how moral claims should affect our responses to the crises of human survival at issue.

1. *Complex.* Something—a fraction, a number, a musical harmony, a machine, a sentence—is complex if it consists of several parts

---

4. Randolph Ryan, "As Slaughter Prevails, Aid Groups Assess Role," *Boston Globe,* May 14, 1994, p. 1. See also the definition offered by the Task Force on Ethical and Legal Issues in Humanitarian Assistance, *The Mohonk Criteria for Humanitarian Assistance in Complex Emergencies* (New York: World Conference on Religion and Peace 1994), 14, n. 1. For discussions of problems associated with such emergencies, see the two special issues of *Medicine and Global Survival* 1, nos. 3–4 (September–December 1994), edited by Jennifer Leaning, M.D., and Lincoln Chen, M.D.

that are connected or woven together.[5] A heap of stones is not complex in this sense, no matter how many stones are part of it, whereas even the simplest living organism beyond the amoeba stage is. Complexity theory studies, among other topics, complex adaptive systems such as human organisms and institutions. A related meaning of the word *complex* is that of something that is difficult to disentangle or analyze, as in a complex logical problem or engineering setup. In none of these circumstances does the word ordinarily carry any moral connotations, having to do with justice or injustice, or good and evil.

Earthquakes, floods, and other natural disasters are often extraordinarily complex, in the sense of exhibiting a number of interacting factors and of confronting both victims and rescuers with excruciatingly difficult choices; yet such disasters are not classified as "complex emergencies" unless human actions are contributing to rendering the resulting crisis more severe. The civil strife in the aftermath of the earthquake in Armenia in 1988, for example, increased the suffering of the quake's victims and rendered assistance efforts more difficult. That crisis would now count as a complex emergency, unlike the aftermath of the earthquake in the Philippines in 1990 or of that in Los Angeles in 1993.

Sometimes the initial images from natural disasters and complex emergencies are too similar for outsiders to tell them apart. Thus news programs conveyed two sets of horrendous images during the third week of January 1995, of buildings toppling, fires raging out of control, people fleeing across streets, fearing for their lives, children being dug out of ruins—after the earthquake in Kobe, Japan, and as a result of the Russian assault on Grozny, the capital of Chechnya. The Japanese earthquake was extraordinarily complex in its own right, with many factors rendering the disaster worse and rescue efforts more difficult. But no one called it a complex emergency. Aid was streaming in from the whole nation and from abroad without risk of assault upon aid workers, and authorities and inhabitants

---

5. The Latin *complexus*, means "plaited together," and the words "plaited together," "interwoven," "connected together" occur variously in dictionary definitions of "complex."

were working together to rescue those trapped and to rebuild. The suffering to the civilian inhabitants of the ravaged Grozny, on the other hand, was largely inflicted by fellow human beings. The city's twelve hospitals were destroyed, and aid workers were at great risk. Calamities thus generated and perpetuated by human beings have, from the outset, ethical dimensions of complexity: dimensions that pertain to moral choices of the most basic kind about how to treat other human beings, and about right and wrong in dealing with them.

This moral aspect of complexity, in complex emergencies, attaches both to causes generating the emergency and to the effort to remedy them. Human undertakings, such as political repression, civil war, or economic pressures from the outside, contribute directly to such a state of crisis, whether or not triggered by a natural disaster. When warring factions, as in Somalia, or governments, as in Sudan or Iraq, not only heighten conditions of famine, migration, and epidemics but also interfere with the distribution of aid, confiscate supplies, and threaten the lives of relief workers, the existing emergency comes to be characterized as complex.

Such a crisis is rendered both more acute and more difficult to overcome to the extent that aid efforts become more dangerous and costly. It involves both unintended and intended causes: on the one hand naturally occurring causes of misery such as drought, famine, epidemics, and overcrowding, and, on the other hand, the purposive interference by public officials, warring groups, or foreign powers with efforts by victims to see to their own survival and by outsiders to come to their aid.

This is not to say that there can ever be absolute demarcations between human and nonhuman causes of emergencies. Famines typically result from mismanagement and maldistribution; earthquakes have very different effects in crowded regions than in deserts. But the difference to which the term *complex* speaks, in this context, is between emergencies where governments or warring factions do and do not contribute directly to societal collapse, do and do not actively threaten the survival of populations.

The moral aspects of such uses of the word *complex*, then, have to do with human activities held to be rightful or wrongful, admirable or reprehensible, just or unjust. Such judgments are unavoidable when the survival of populations is at issue. But the very complexity of the causes of the emergencies makes the attribution of responsibility complex as well. As a result, the contestants on each side of the related conflicts often levy accusations at outsiders as well as at adversaries.

The eighteenth-century philosopher David Hume wrote of conditions in which survival is threatened on a large scale as ones in which justice itself may be out of reach.[6] He pointed to both natural and human causes of such a state of affairs. Justice can be expected, first of all, only in an intermediate range with respect to both natural scarcity and human failures. If there is such scarcity that human survival is impossible, then justice is to no avail. Conversely, if there is utter abundance of all that human beings might need, justice is unnecessary. Second, justice is only within reach and needed when human beings are neither so demoniacally evil and shortsightedly blind to future consequences that appeals to justice are to no avail, nor so uniformly generous, altruistic, kind, and foresightful that problems or disputes would never arise.

When Hume wrote, there would have been no way for him to conceive of humanly inflicted suffering on the massive scale that we now witness. The world's population had not yet reached 1 billion. The armaments of the time could inflict but a fraction of the casualties that accrue in contemporary wars. And reports of threats to survival in distant lands made their way slowly, if at all, to the European public. But if Hume could have foreseen a complex emergency such as that in Rwanda in 1994–1995, he might have seen it as an example of conditions in which any sort of justice is undercut by the interweaving of human and natural forces at their most lethal: where political strife amounting to genocide, along with hunger, lack of water, epidemics, and agricultural failure, threatens millions of women, children, and men, in addition to those killed from the outset, and also poses extraordinary risks for those attempting humanitarian assistance.

6. *An Enquiry Concerning the Principles of Morals* (1751; Indianapolis: Hackett Publishing Co., 1983), section III, part I.

As Judith Shklar points out, however, in *The Faces of Injustice*, the distinction between humanly inflicted injustices and naturally occurring misfortunes such as those from earthquakes comes more easily for outsiders than for the victims themselves: "[T]he difference between misfortune and injustice frequently involves our willingness and our capacity to act or not to act on behalf of the victims, to blame or to absolve, to help, mitigate, and compensate, or just to turn away."[7]

The concept of a *complex* emergency was not available as recently as 1990, when Shklar wrote. But it, too, is peculiarly a concept coined from the perspective of outsiders. To be in the midst of calamities like those experienced by victims of such emergencies is to be beset in such ways that distinctions between human and nonhuman causes, moral and nonmoral factors, are of little or no avail.

2. *Emergency.* An emergency is defined as a "juncture that arises or turns up; especially a state of things unexpectedly arising and urgently demanding immediate action"; or as a situation "of great danger that develops suddenly and unexpectedly."[8] Yet the vast and many-dimensional threats to human survival labeled as "complex emergencies" do not altogether fit these dictionary definitions of emergencies. A landslide, an earthquake, a flood may come about in such a sudden and unexpected way; but the crisis in Rwanda, though it ignited with sudden force, was not unexpected; and the famine resulting from civil war in Somalia was less and less unexpected as the months wore on.

Such situations are, however, emergencies in that they are "urgently demanding action." They are viewed, therefore, as emergencies in a sense that is primarily moral or valuational: namely a situation so serious as to have priority over others. Just as emergency vehicles have priority on the road and other cars must pull to the side and let them pass, so the claim for complex emergencies is that they represent such desperate human predicaments that they must receive priority over other human needs. Funds allocated elsewhere

7. *The Faces of Injustice* (New Haven: Yale University Press, 1990), 2.
8. *Oxford English Dictionary; American Heritage Dictionary.*

by donor agencies and nations must be reallocated, at least for the short run.

The use of the word *emergency* to indicate priority in the distribution of resources constitutes, therefore, an implicit moral claim. Unless it is seen and evaluated as such, it can serve to bypass issues of weighing and comparing responses: Why, for instance, rush to provide aid at one time rather than earlier or later? Why bring aid to one society and not to another in similar straits? How long should the aid continue, and at what costs to all involved? Merely labeling some crises and not others as "emergencies" ought not to be dispositive with respect to where to rush assistance on an emergency basis.

Here again, as with the distinction between "complex" and other emergencies or disasters, the distinction between complex crises that count and do not count as emergencies is one made from the perspective of outsiders who must decide how and when to try to be of help, rather than from that of the victims themselves, for whom any threat to life is an emergency, even if no outsider learns of their predicament or comes to their help. Many instances of vast human suffering have gone largely unnoticed by those who might have come to the rescue, or, to the extent noticed and documented, have elicited little outside response. Idi Amin's reign of terror in Uganda in the 1970s, in which over 300,000 persons were killed, would have constituted, in today's terms, a "complex emergency." But would it have been granted priority at the time by the international community? And how might such an expression have applied to the Nazi Holocaust? Or to the Chinese famine of 1959–1961, now estimated to have taken between 20 and 40 million lives? Too often, what is at stake is not so much the levels of human suffering as whether or not the outside world becomes aware of this suffering and chooses to make an issue of it.

One must distinguish, then, between collective human emergencies as experienced from within and from without. From within, they count as such whether or not aid is available—and indeed, as mentioned above, whether or not the suffering is inflicted on purpose by human forces or not. For victims, likewise, the question of whether their suffering is increased because of embargoes, sanctions, or other forms of economic warfare imposed by outside governments is also harder to assess than for outsiders. The more ruthless the regime at the receiving end of such measures, the more likely it is to expose its own people to the worst hardships resulting from them, and thus to contribute to what outsiders view as a more severe complex emergency than would otherwise have been the case.

Media coverage, moreover, may careen from one emergency to another, while leaving some out altogether, depending, in part, on how difficult it is for reporters and photographers to gain entry into particular societies—into Somalia, say, rather than the Sudan in 1993. The more ruthlessly a regime controls entry and exit, the less likely it is that adequate documentation of the emergency by outsiders will be possible. And with governments and aid organizations competing for media attention to particular crises, the coverage becomes even more erratic, from the victims' point of view.

To sum up, the question of what constitutes a "complex emergency" has both factual and moral aspects. The factual aspects concern the conditions in a particular society in crisis and the magnitude of the needs to be met. The moral aspects have to do with how the determination is to be made that such an emergency exists, where responsibilities should be assigned, what kind of priority should be accorded the effort to seek remedies, and how long the state of emergency should occupy center stage if aid efforts do not bear fruit. When the moral aspects are not kept clearly in sight, it is likely that they will be blurred and thought, erroneously, to go without saying so long as factual answers are found to the question. Such confusion is especially likely to come about whenever *humanitarian*, with its seemingly self-evident moral import, is used in conjunction with *complex* and *emergency*.

Humanitarian

The term *humanitarian*, unlike *complex* and *emergency*, has immediate moral connotations. It evokes helpfulness, benevolence, and humane concern going to all who are in need, without regard to person.

A recent definition holds that a humanitarian is "one devoted to the promotion of human welfare and the advancement of social reforms; a philanthropist."[9] Such a person is admired even by many who are less altruistic. So are many forms of humanitarian assistance, even by those who regard particular undertakings so described as poorly planned or executed.

This positive view of humanitarians was less prevalent in the nineteenth century, however, when the word first came into common usage in English. The adjective *humanitarian* was then used, according to the *Oxford English Dictionary*, in a manner "nearly always contemptuous, connoting one who goes to excess in humane principles." The word conveyed deep-rooted suspicion, unlike such words as *humane, kindly,* or *good*. At the time, the relation of *humanitarian* to *humane* was often seen as similar to that of today's *do-gooder* to *good*. Many regarded those laying claims to humanitarianism as at best woolly-headed and sentimental about humanity at large, propounding vast schemes for human improvement even as they neglected their responsibilities to their own families and communities, and at worst as persons using the mantle of humanitarianism and the love of humankind to cover up for every form of religious, commercial, even criminal abuse and exploitation of others.

Charles Dickens's portrait of Mr. Pecksniff, in *Martin Chuzzlewit*, conveys that form of exploitative hypocrisy so perfectly that "pecksniffian" has entered the English language. Pecksniff, a self-proclaimed "humanitarian philosopher," expresses unctuous concern for all of humanity, giving his own daughters (and fellow parasites until he betrays them) the names Mercy and Charity. He is shown up for the scoundrel he is, scheming to defraud and torment his fellow humans while intoning the language of universal love.

By the twentieth century, a great shift in the meaning of *humanitarian* was taking place: one that matters as we seek to understand current conflicts about when and how to respond to complex humanitarian emergencies. The term has come to be more focused and less derogatory. It is more focused, in that it concerns specifically the effort to meet fundamental human needs and to alleviate suffering,

9. *American Heritage Dictionary.*

rather than all conceivable efforts to improve the human condition. And it is less derogatory, in that suspicion is no longer part of the reaction it evokes for most people. A humanitarian, rather, is seen as someone genuinely concerned to meet urgent human needs wherever they arise, without distinction as to nationality, ethnic background, or religion.

Early in our century, Dr. Albert Schweitzer helped to dramatize the personal choice that taking such humanitarianism seriously represents. His writings on religion and music had already achieved wide recognition in Europe when he went, in 1913, to Gabon, in what was then French Equatorial Africa, in order to build a hospital and minister to those most in need of help. In explaining how he had come to make this choice, Schweitzer wrote that he had read about "the physical miseries of the natives in the virgin forests; . . . and the more I thought about it, the stranger it seemed to me that we Europeans trouble ourselves so little about the great humanitarian task which offers itself to us in far-off lands."[10]

In answer to the question "Am I my brother's keeper?" Schweitzer reputedly answered: "How could I not be? I cannot escape my responsibility." He insisted that all human beings counted as brothers, in this sense: his obligation was to help those in need, wherever he found them, to the best of his ability. By the end of our century, however, and in no small part because of the complex emergencies now endangering the survival of so many, the term *humanitarian* has undergone yet another shift. It is a shift not yet noted, to the best of my knowledge, in any dictionaries. With the growth of U.N. aid agencies, of nongovernmental assistance programs, and of so many governmental and intergovernmental efforts designated as humanitarian, the word no longer denotes only persons who work to alleviate suffering and to meet human needs, nor only their attitudes, beliefs, or actions. It now concerns, also, collective assistance programs in the name of the international community, such as those of the United Nations, which created a Department of Humanitarian Affairs in 1992. But in the process, the term has expanded still further: it has come to concern not only the

10. *On the Edge of the Primeval Forest* (London: A. and C. Black, 1922).

provision of aid, by governments, nongovernmental organizations, and individuals, but also the predicament of those persons and communities and populations who are in greatest need of such aid. Accordingly, when we now speak of "humanitarian crises," or of "complex humanitarian emergencies," we have in mind the crises for those who are afflicted as well as for those who are coming to their aid or considering doing so.

But this expansion in the meaning of *humanitarian* brings with it a renewal of the nineteenth-century suspicions as to motives, especially when governments or large groups are invoking the need for humanitarian assistance. This time, the suspicion is directed both to governments or groups calling for aid and to those providing it. Leaders of states receiving humanitarian aid or heads of factions in a civil war may extort a proportion of funds, food, and medical supplies for their personal enrichment or for use by their own troops; governments and groups providing aid may mismanage the funds allocated to them. The larger the number of persons involved, the greater the potential for miscalculation, corruption, and abuse.

The suspicion regarding motives is especially natural when it comes to the escalation, in the 1990s, of military interventions on humanitarian grounds. Throughout history, the vast majority of invasions, proxy wars, and political coups engineered from the outside have been undertaken for self-serving, often expansionist reasons quite different from any humanitarian goals invoked by their sponsors. A case in point is Hitler's claim, on September 23, 1938, that ethnic Germans and various nationalities in Czechoslovakia were being maltreated to the point that the security of more than 3 million human beings was at stake.[11]

By now, the term *humanitarian intervention* is more frequently invoked for what appear to be at least in part genuinely altruistic undertakings.[12] And the criteria are changing with respect to when

---

11. See Thomas M. Franck and Nigel S. Rodley, "After Bangladesh: The Law of Humanitarian Intervention by Military Force," *American Journal of International Law* 67 (1973): 275–305.

12. See David J. Scheffer, "Toward a Modern Doctrine of Humanitarian Intervention," *University of Toledo Law Review* 23 (winter 1992): 293. For a discussion of mixed

and how it is seen as legitimate to intervene in the affairs of a state and across national frontiers to deliver humanitarian aid. But when it comes to justifications offered for military interventions on humanitarian grounds, the original nineteenth-century suspicion of claims to humanitarianism stands as a caution against idealistic labels that risk concealing or developing into old-fashioned power politics.

It is against the background of these shifts in the meaning of *humanitarian* and of the vast expansion of humanitarian operations that a growing sense of unease, even anguish, is being voiced by individuals providing aid and health care or monitoring human rights in the midst of crises such as the Rwandan civil war. These individuals have no reason to doubt their own motives; often inspired by such figures as Albert Schweitzer or Florence Nightingale, they have gone into the field prepared to undergo hardship and to sacrifice much in their personal lives in order to be of service. They knowingly risk illness, exhaustion, sometimes even kidnapping and death, as witness the many human rights workers murdered the world over in recent years. But what has come to trouble some of them far more is the sense that the humanitarian aid they are providing in certain crises may be used in part to feed soldiers, enrich warlords, and prolong conflicts, thus adding to human suffering rather than diminishing its sway.

A debate concerning these risks of contributing to doing harm, even through efforts to be of help in an extreme humanitarian emergency, came to a head in 1994 among the different sections of Médecins Sans Frontières (MSF)—the organization of health professionals originally known as the "French doctors" and now comprising members from a great many other nations—working in Rwandan refugee camps in Tanzania and Zaire. The refugees in these camps were Hutus, including participants in what may fairly be called genocide, resulting in the killing of what may have been

---

motives in interventions, see Michael Walzer, *Just and Unjust Wars* (New York: Basic Books, 1977), and Jarat Chopra and Thomas G. Weiss, "Sovereignty Is No Longer Sacrosanct: Codifying Humanitarian Intervention," *Ethics and International Affairs* 6 (1992): 95–117.

half a million Tutsis. According to the MSF, the Hutu leaders domi-
nated the refugee camps, conducted police operations and military
training, and ordered the murder of fellow refugees seeking to be
repatriated. The French section of MSF chose to withdraw from the
camps—an anguished decision, considering that its members knew
they were thereby abandoning children and other persons innocent
of all wrongdoing. They asked, in speaking of "the ambiguity of
humanitarian aid":

> Is it acceptable for the international community to not only ignore the
> reality existing in the camps, but to directly contribute to the coercion
> and manipulation of a population by giving legitimacy and means
> to a leadership accused of perpetrating genocide? Is it acceptable to
> continue to support a "sanctuary" from which a military force can
> launch an attack on Rwanda, and perhaps finish the genocide that
> they commenced in April?[13]

The Dutch section of MSF decided to stay, along with other organizations. But all recognized the acuteness of the moral dilemmas
regarding providing aid under such conditions. For those who work
for aid agencies as among those who work for donor governments,
there is growing awareness of these dilemmas. How can they best
respond to today's complex humanitarian emergencies, so different
from the circumstances in which individual humanitarian workers
carried out their mission in the past? The opportunities to save lives,
to nourish, and to heal are unprecedented, given the resources now
available and the networks that have sprung up for utilizing them.
But the traps and risks of doing harm are greater than ever as well. As
Rony Brauman, former president of MSF, puts it: "Never in history
have so many lives been saved, so much distress been alleviated,
thanks to a movement with greater vitality and public support than
ever. Rarely in history has humanitarian aid been marked by such
ambiguities—the reverse of the brilliant medal of its success."[14]

These ambiguities are exacerbated, Brauman indicates, by the
scope of today's humanitarian campaigns, the media attention for

---

13. Médecins Sans Frontières, "Rwanda: The Limits and Ambiguity of Humanitarian Aid," report, Paris, 1994.

14. *L'Action humanitaire* (Paris: Flammarion, 1994), 79. My translation.

which providers compete, and the involvement of military forces either to render aid or to protect those who do. These are elements of complexity that humanitarians such as Albert Schweitzer had no need to take into account.

Least of all, perhaps, could these humanitarians have foreseen a problem that has arisen with special acuteness in the conflicts in Rwanda and Bosnia: whether to give priority to humanitarian assistance or to the protection of human rights—to strive for reconciliation and healing or for justice. It is often possible to strive for both at once. But if the choice is between bringing those guilty of ethnic cleansing and mass murder to justice or negotiating a quicker end to violence by granting them amnesty, which is it to be? And once war is over, should amnesty be granted and resources focused on development, or should they go, also, to war crimes trials?

Human Rights

Today's humanitarian crises challenge our most fundamental assumptions about the responses that human rights violations demand. In Chapter 2, above, I have cited the documentation by Dorothy Jones of the slow shift, in the course of this century, of talk about human rights from early dismissal as sheer rhetoric to partial implementation, in Eastern Europe, South Africa, South Korea, the Philippines, and so many other societies. But an important difference between these human rights successes and the many contemporary failures has to do with the patterns of *state* violation of human rights against which Dorothy Jones rightly saw human rights advocacy as having been partially successful; we now witness vast and growing violations in regions where not only states but many of the most basic forms of governance are collapsing.

In a speech given in 1993, Ian Martin, secretary-general of Amnesty International from 1986 to 1992, describes the changes in perception that have taken place even in the few years since Dorothy Jones wrote. As we read newspaper reports from Bosnia and so many other beleaguered regions, he points out, we find that these reports are not just reports of *someone* being imprisoned, tortured, or executed, and not now most commonly because the victim's opinions or religion are unacceptable to the *government*. [Emphasis added.] Open your newspaper any day now and you will find a report from somewhere in the world of hundreds of thousands of people being killed, raped, forced from their homes, driven into poverty and starvation, because there is no government able to control the situation in their country, or because there no longer is a country with accepted borders.[15]

When nonexistent or enfeebled governments cannot be held accountable for violations of rights of citizens, then who is thus accountable? The time-honored method of letter-writing campaigns to public authorities asking for the release of particular prisoners of conscience is beside the point in today's humanitarian emergencies. These emergencies challenge us to consider the most fundamental and long-standing conceptions of human rights and how they relate to what obligations are called for in response.

One such conception, underlying many contemporary human rights claims, is stated in the preamble of the U.N. Charter and the first article of the Universal Declaration of Human Rights: that all human beings, regardless of culture and history, are born free and equal and have inherent dignity. For many, this statement reflects a religious worldview in which God has created human beings thus free and equal, with inherent dignity. For others, fundamental human equality in its own right underlies claims to dignity and rights. Fang Lizhi, the Chinese astrophysicist and human rights advocate, states the latter sort of linkage between premise and rights as follows: "Like all members of the human race, the Chinese are born with a body and a brain, with passions and a soul. *Therefore* [emphasis added] they can and must enjoy the same inalienable rights, dignity, and liberty, as all other human beings."[16]

Fang Lizhi is making a legitimate claim upon his own government. But what happens to his *"Therefore"* when, for mounting

15. "The New World Order: Opportunity or Threat for Human Rights?" lecture, April 14, 1993, Harvard Law School Human Rights Program.

16. Quoted by John Shattuck in "The Human Rights Watch," *Boston Globe*, December 10, 1994, p. 11.

millions of people, there is no state to be held accountable for failures to respect such rights? How is the linkage between the right to equality and the responsibility not to violate it to be upheld? What are our obligations to victimized strangers under such circumstances? The language of family or of brotherhood, familiar since biblical times, carries with it a view regarding universal responsibility that the sheer expression of equality does not easily muster on its own. But what does it mean to be our brothers' keepers in today's world? What obligations do we have toward all of humanity, considered as part of our family, and what entitlements do all its members have? Does the size of the presumed family matter in this regard? Should it matter? Two thousand years ago, there were perhaps 100 million people on Earth, most of them unknown to people living in any one community. Even then, the language of universal brotherhood was rarely adhered to in practice. What practical force does this language have today, when we are nearing 6 billion inhabitants on Earth, with 1.3 billion in extreme need, many of them children, many unable to survive without outside help?

Contemporary writers have done much to illuminate the complex theoretical relationships among rights, needs, responsibilities, and obligations.[17] But they, too, have generally considered rights within a framework of states that are to be held accountable for upholding basic rights; among those thinkers who considered the rights of the needy abroad, most did not yet know of the present escalation of conflict, population, and human need. Thus Henry Shue argued,

17. See, for recent works on the theory of rights, Annette Baier, "Claims, Rights, Responsibilities," in Gene Outka and John P. Reeder, eds., *Prospects for a Common Morality* (Princeton: Princeton University Press, 1993), 149–69; Jack Donnelly, *Universal Human Rights* (Ithaca: Cornell University Press, 1989); Ronald Dworkin, *Taking Rights Seriously* (Cambridge: Harvard University Press, 1977); Mary Ann Glendon, *Rights Talk: The Impoverishment of Political Discourse* (New York: Free Press, 1991); Stanley Hoffmann, *Duties beyond Borders* (Syracuse: Syracuse University Press, 1981); Onora O'Neill, *Faces of Hunger: An Essay on Poverty, Justice, and Development* (London: Allen and Unwin, 1986); the essays in Stephen Shute and Susan Hurley, eds., *On Human Rights: The Oxford Amnesty Lectures 1993* (New York: Basic Books, 1993); Henry Shue, *Basic Rights* (Princeton: Princeton University Press, 1980); Judith Jarvis Thomson, *The Realm of Rights* (Cambridge: Harvard University Press, 1990); Lloyd Weinreb, *Oedipus at Fenway Park: What Rights Are and Why There Are Any* (Cambridge: Harvard University Press, 1994).

in 1980, that subsistence rights—to unpolluted air and water, adequate food, clothing, shelter, and minimum preventive public health care—are among the basic rights that are "everyone's minimum reasonable demands upon the rest of humanity." The duty to make the requisite sacrifices should fall, in the first place, on the affluent, on account of "the principle that degrading inequalities ought to be avoided."[18] If asked, fifteen years later, how his views should apply to the massive humanitarian crises we are now facing, Shue might find himself as perplexed as are many in the human rights community who operate with simpler premises of equal rights, common humanity, or brotherhood.

More recently, John Rawls has offered a different set of premises for human rights in his essay "The Law of Peoples," to address the problem of what to do about rights in "outlaw states" and in societies in disarray. Rawls specifies that his account of human rights does not rely on any universal premises such as those expressed by Fang Lizhi or Henry Shue. It does not postulate any comprehensive view such as that all human beings have equal worth or have certain moral or intellectual powers entitling them to such rights. Nor does Rawls claim that his account is based on notions of universal brotherhood or family, an all-encompassing social contract, or any other universal obligations. Instead, he takes a constructivist approach, building outward from "well-ordered societies." Basic human rights, such as those to life, to a modicum of liberty, to property, and to formal justice, constitute, for Rawls, "a minimum standard of well-ordered political institutions for all people who belong, as members in good standing, to a just political society of peoples."[19]

What about the longer list of rights contained in the Universal Declaration of Human Rights and in that affirmed in Vienna in 1993? Some rights in that list are more realistically viewed as aspirational, Rawls suggests. But how, then, should those fortunate enough to live in well-ordered societies envisage the rights of those who do not? And in particular the rights of peoples in regions such as the former Yugoslavia or Rwanda?

18. Shue, *Basic Rights*, 19, 119.
19. "The Law of Peoples," in Shute and Hurley, eds., *On Human Rights*, 41–82, at 68.

Their fate, Rawls holds, has to be the subject of concern for people in the well-ordered societies who enjoy the assurance of basic human rights; but those less fortunate have no specific claim on those who are better off, nor do the latter appear to have specific obligations in return. The former have, first of all, no claims of a redistributive kind, no matter how miserable they may be. Rawls specifically asserts that the difference principle, which functions within a well-ordered state as a redistributive mechanism, is not feasible as a way to deal with what he terms "unfavorable conditions" among societies—that is, societies that lack the cultural and political traditions and other factors that make well-ordered societies possible. In that case, what obligations flow, for Rawls, from such a view of human rights?

> The ideal conception of the society of peoples that well-ordered societies affirm directs that in due course all societies must reach, or be assisted to, the conditions that make a well-ordered society possible. This implies that human rights are to be recognized and secured everywhere and that basic human needs are to be met.[20]

Rawls's use of the passive tense only highlights the problem with respect to accountability. Human rights "are to be recognized and secured everywhere" and "basic human needs are to be met." Yet the magnitude of the calamities that we confront today offers the starkest challenge to the premises underlying human rights claims that issue only in such language, just as much as it challenges the premises underlying the language of universal brotherhood. Where *should* the responsibility fall for securing rights and meeting needs for the many millions whose survival is now at risk?

Whose Responsibility?

With complex humanitarian emergencies, the problem is to find methods that can be used to uphold human rights, and to find

---

20. Ibid., 76.

*ways of living up to the obligation to uphold—without getting
killed by the oppressors in the process.*

Jennifer Leaning, M.D.

As the images multiply of unspeakable suffering, outsiders anguish over how best to allocate aid and to weigh the costs, even in human terms, of attempting to carry out such aid. They anguish, too, at the contrast between the inestimable worth many are willing to grant to each life and their awareness—made so much more immediate by television coverage—of the burden of suffering under which so many fellow human beings labor.[21] Most people care more about the survival of at least some—themselves, their family and friends, often also their fellow citizens—than about the rest of humanity. Yet many also take seriously the challenge posed by views such as those of Albert Schweitzer and worry about the injustice in treating human beings differently on such grounds.

Henry Sidgwick, the British nineteenth-century thinker, found this contrast to be serious enough to threaten any coherent view of ethics. On the one hand, he was prepared, as a utilitarian, to hold as the fundamental principle of ethics "the principle that another's greater good is to be preferred to one's own lesser good." According to such a principle, any sacrifice on one's own part would be called for, so long as it could achieve a greater good for others.[22] And to those who urged that we owe more to our fellow citizens than to the rest of humanity, Sidgwick responded that he had never seen, nor could even "conceive, any ethical reasoning that will provide even a plausible basis" for such a view.[23] On the other hand, Sidgwick also took for granted what he called the commonsense view that our obligations to help others differ depending on the relationships in which we stand to them:

21. See Sissela Bok, *Secrets: On the Ethics of Concealment and Revelation* (New York: Pantheon Books, 1982), 102–15, for a discussion of the factors entering into this contrast.

22. "Some Fundamental Ethical Controversies," *Mind*, o.s. 14 (1889): 473–87, at 474.

23. *Practical Ethics* (London: Swan Sonnenschein and Co., 1898), 68.

We should all agree that each of us is bound to show kindness to his parents and spouse and children, and to other kinsmen in a less degree; and to those who have rendered services to him, and any others whom he may have admitted to his intimacy and called friends; and to neighbors and to fellow-countrymen more than others; and perhaps we may say to those of our own race more than to black or yellow men, and generally to human beings in proportion to their affinity to ourselves.[24]

A metaphor that has often been used, beginning in antiquity, to convey the conflict to which Sidgwick points, is that of concentric circles of human concern and allegiance, with the self in the center, surrounded by circles for family members, friends, community members, fellow citizens, and the rest of humanity.[25] The circle metaphor speaks to the necessary tensions between what is owed to insiders and what to outsiders of the many interlocking groups in which we all exist. The metaphor has long been used either to urge us to stretch our concern outward from the narrowest personal confines toward the needs of outsiders, strangers, all of humanity,[26] or to stress a contrasting view: that of "my station and its duties," according to which at least some of our primary allegiances are, precisely, dependent on our situation and role in life and cannot be overridden by obligations to humanity at large.

24. *The Methods of Ethics,* 6th ed. (1906; New York: Dover Publications, 1966), 246.

25. See, for example, Hierocles, cited in A. A. Long and D. N. Sedley, *The Hellenistic Philosophers* (Cambridge: Cambridge University Press, 1987), 1:349–50. For a consideration of this view in the context of contemporary choices between universal and more localized allegiances, see Martha Nussbaum, "Patriotism or Cosmopolitanism?" *Boston Review* 19 (October/November 1994): 3–6, with replies by twenty-nine persons including myself. For a discussion of the circle metaphor in the context of the responsibility of the affluent to meet subsistence needs of the most deprived, across all boundaries and regions of such circles, see Shue, *Basic Rights,* 134–38.

26. Sometimes the circle metaphor has also been intended to expand to include animals, as Peter Singer holds in *The Expanding Circle* (New York: Farrar, Strauss, Giroux, 1981). This was also the intent of Albert Schweitzer, who maintained that it was not possible for anyone espousing his principle of reverence for life to draw a line between humans and animals. See Schweitzer, *Out of My Life and Thought* (1931), trans. A. B. Lemke (New York: Henry Holt and Co., 1990), 235: "The ethic of reverence for Life is the ethic of Love widened into universality."

The first view corresponds to universalist humanitarianism in many of its forms. It is expressed in statements such as that by Schweitzer, above. Saying that all are brothers is also saying that the boundaries of the different circles should count for little when it comes to helping those in need. The second view, which emphasizes those boundaries and stresses the priority of directly experienced allegiances over far-flung ones, echoes in the second of the passages from Sidgwick quoted above. Both the universalist and the graduated view concern human survival and security, no matter how thoroughly advocates of these views suspect opponents of parochialism, hypocrisy, or blindness to genuine human need.

Reasonable exponents of both views agree at least that one ought to help others when this does not mean shortchanging persons in need to whom one has preexisting obligations. They agree, further, that certain prohibitions, as on killing and breaking promises and cheating, ought to hold across all the boundaries of all the circles; and that basic requirements of fairness are due, likewise, to all. Many also join in agreeing that in certain acute emergencies, such as those following an earthquake, the obligation to offer humanitarian aid across boundaries should supersede needs that can wait. It is when the needs of outsiders are of vast extent and prolonged duration and would constitute a considerable reallocation of scarce resources that holders of the graduated view are most likely to balk at the use of the term *emergency* to urge priority for such needs over the needs of family members or compatriots.

No matter from which perspective we view the image of the concentric circles, it matters to strive to see the importance of the other perspective and to recognize the role that both play in conflicts over how to respond to the surge in complex humanitarian emergencies. In so doing, it matters, too, to sort out the factual and moral controversies inherent in the concept of "complex humanitarian emergencies." It is too easy, otherwise, to ignore either perspective: either to fail to explore the important empirical questions about how such crises arise and what strategies are most appropriate to meet existing needs and prevent recurrences of the crises, or to ignore the genuine moral ambivalence many feel regarding the conflicting calls on their concern and on their sense of responsibility. To the extent that we fail to keep such distinctions in mind, and to explore their ramifications, we risk answering too hastily the strategic and moral questions that today's vast humanitarian crises have raised with unprecedented starkness, and that will be the crucial moral questions for the coming century.

When it comes to practical responses to such crises, it is as short-sighted to fail to take seriously moral factors as to leave strategic ones out of account. (See Chapter 4.) In the absence of fuller perception of both, with due respect for their complexity, international responses to complex emergencies peter out in confusion, at times backfire. In Bosnia as in Rwanda, both sets of considerations would have dictated efforts at prevention instead of the blunders and short-sighted policies that helped precipitate the crisis.

The sense of hopelessness that many voice at seeing the spread of humanitarian emergencies, and the inadequacy, to date, of efforts to cope with them, is nevertheless premature. To reverse the present development may well take work by as many persons and groups, on as many fronts, and with as much ingenuity and courage, as went into the work against segregation, apartheid, and the nuclear balance of terror of which Martin Luther King, Jr., spoke in the passage cited at the beginning of this chapter. In 1964, too, many were ready to give up all hope of peaceful resolutions to those evils. Three decades later, we have more reason than ever to heed his conclusion:

> I have the audacity to believe that peoples everywhere can have three meals a day for their bodies, education and culture for their minds, and dignity, equality, and freedom for their spirits. I still believe we shall overcome.

Index of Names